THE VISUAL DICTIONARY *of*
SHIPS *and* SAILING

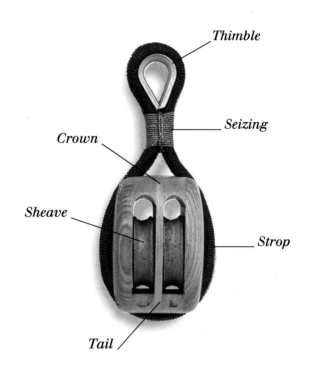

Thimble

Seizing

Crown

Sheave

Strop

Tail

A STROPPED BLOCK

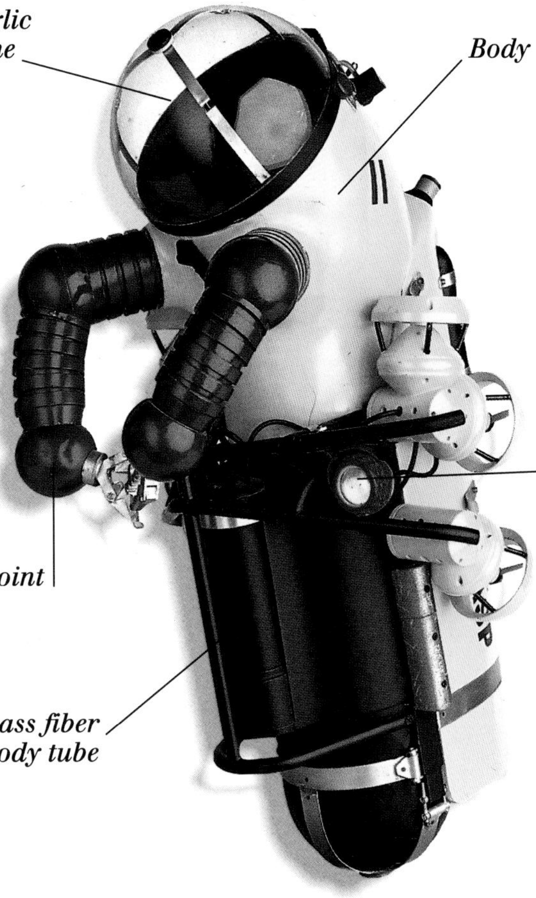

ONE-MAN DIVING SUIT

Acrylic dome

Body casting

Lynx helicopter

Wrist joint

Light

Glass fiber body tube

FRIGATE HMS ALACRITY

Seacat missile launcher

Funnel

Mast

Gun turret

F174

SONAR bulge

BOW OF A 74-GUN SHIP

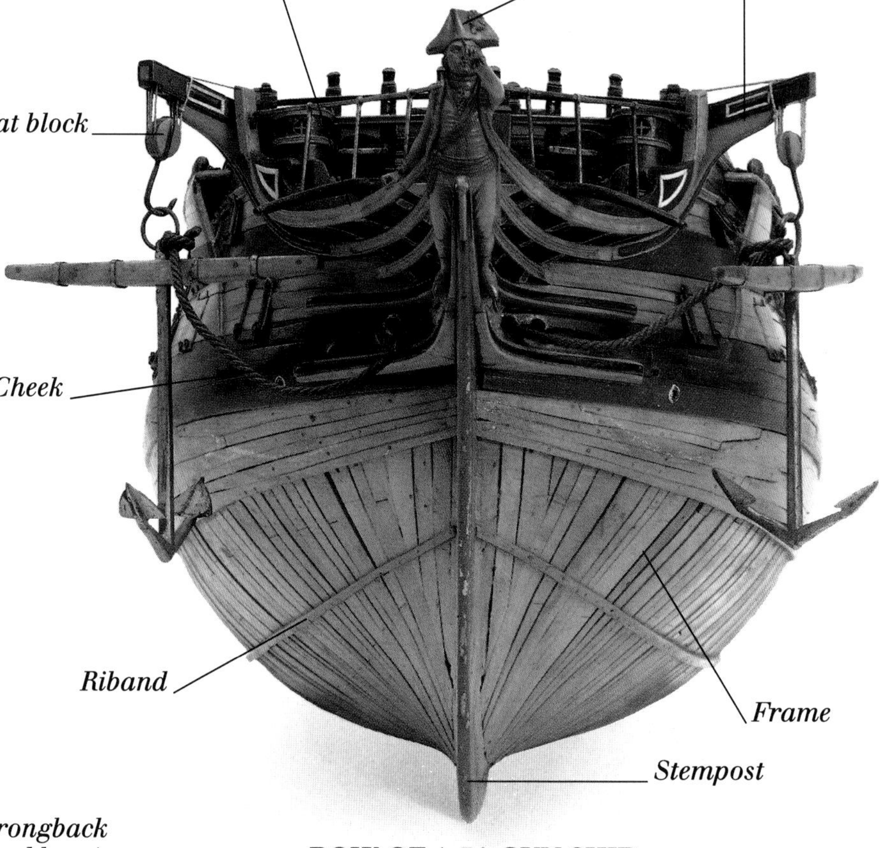

Main rail

Figurehead

Supporter

Cat block

Cheek

Riband

Frame

Stempost

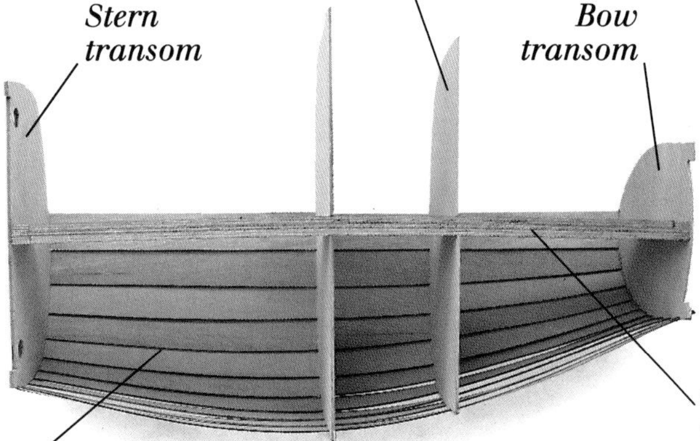

DINGHY JIG WITH PLANKING

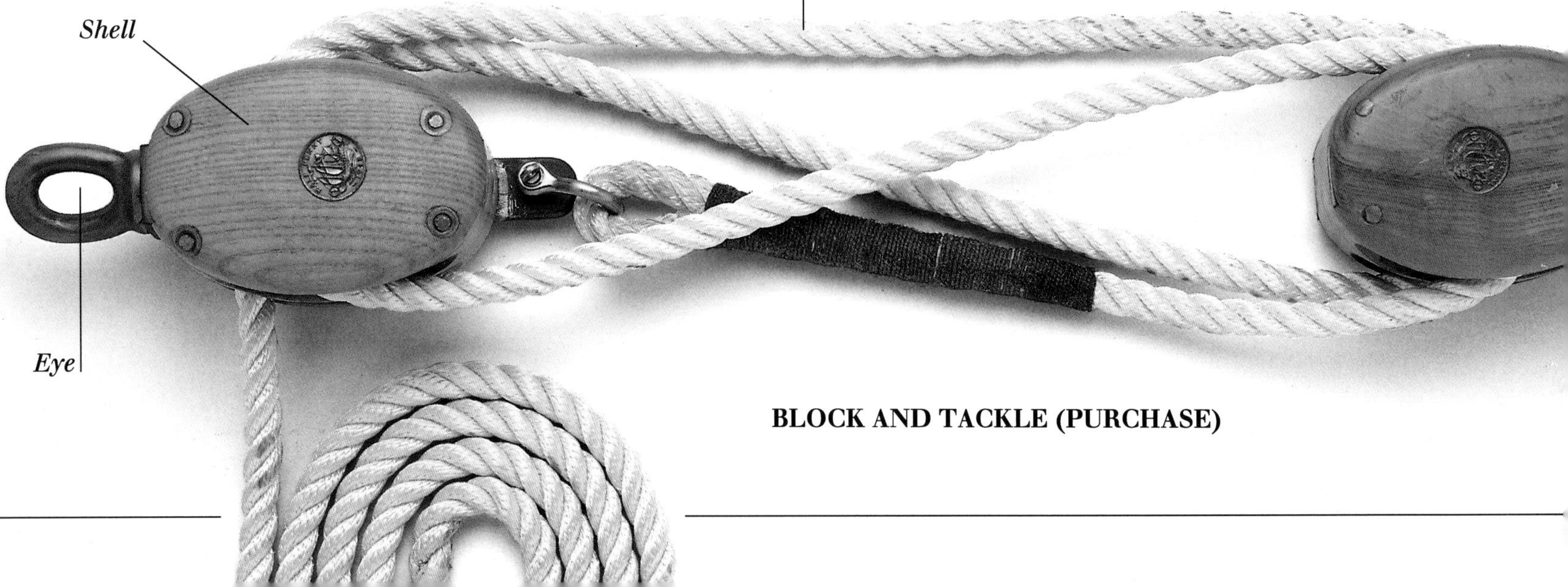

Station mold

Stern transom

Bow transom

Strake

Strongback (backbone)

BLOCK AND TACKLE (PURCHASE)

Running part

Shell

Eye

EYEWITNESS VISUAL DICTIONARIES

THE VISUAL DICTIONARY *of*
SHIPS *and* SAILING

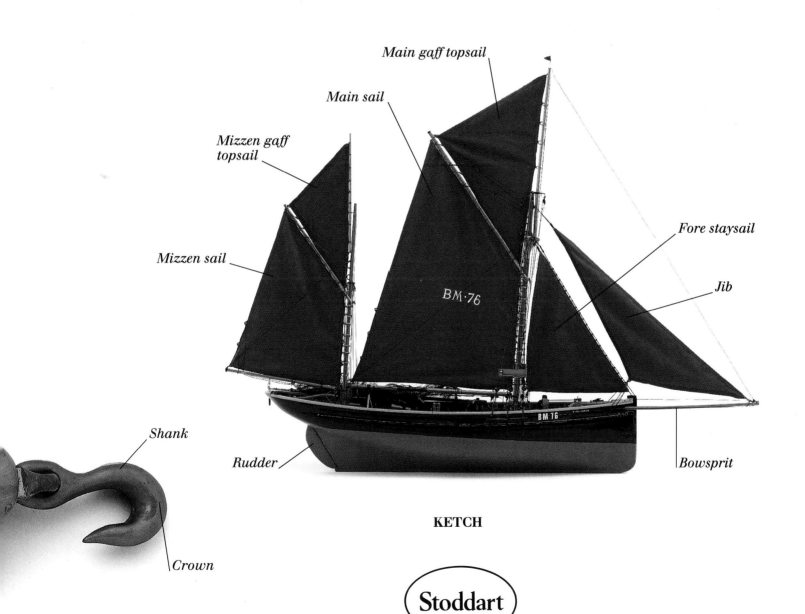

Main gaff topsail

Main sail

Mizzen gaff topsail

Mizzen sail

Fore staysail

Jib

BM·76

BM 76

Shank

Rudder

Bowsprit

Crown

KETCH

Stoddart

A DORLING KINDERSLEY BOOK

PROJECT ART EDITOR STEPHEN KNOWLDEN
DESIGN ASSISTANT PAUL CALVER

PROJECT EDITOR ROGER TRITTON

SERIES ART EDITOR PAUL WILKINSON
ART DIRECTOR CHEZ PICTHALL
MANAGING EDITOR RUTH MIDGLEY

PHOTOGRAPHY JAMES STEVENSON, DAVE KING, STEVE GORTON, TIM RIDLEY

PRODUCTION HILARY STEPHENS

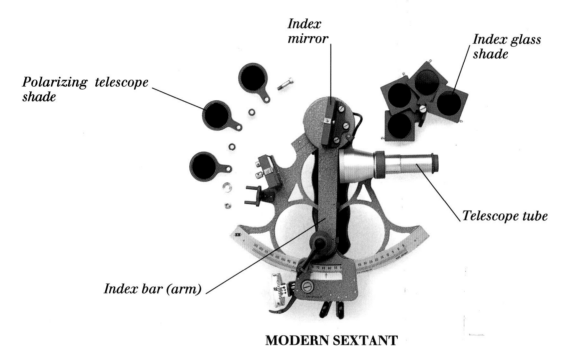

Polarizing telescope shade

Index mirror

Index glass shade

Telescope tube

Index bar (arm)

MODERN SEXTANT

PUBLISHED IN CANADA IN 1991 BY
STODDART PUBLISHING CO. LIMITED
34 LESMILL ROAD, TORONTO, CANADA
M3B 2T6

FIRST PUBLISHED IN GREAT BRITAIN IN 1991 BY DORLING KINDERSLEY LIMITED,
9 HENRIETTA STREET, LONDON WC2E 8PS

CANADIAN CATALOGUING IN PUBLICATION DATA
MAIN ENTRY UNDER TITLE:
THE VISUAL DICTIONARY OF SHIPS AND SAILING
(EYEWITNESS VISUAL DICTIONARIES)
INCLUDES BIBLIOGRAPHICAL REFERENCES AND INDEX.
ISBN 0-7737-2547-4

1. SHIPS - PICTORIAL WORKS - JUVENILE LITERATURE.
2. SHIPS - TERMINOLOGY - JUVENILE LITERATURE.
3. PICTURE DICTIONARIES, ENGLISH - JUVENILE
LITERATURE. I. SERIES.

VM150.V57 1991   j387.2'03   C91-094398-2

REPRODUCED BY GRB GRAFICA, VERONA, ITALY
PRINTED AND BOUND BY ARNOLDO MONDADORI, VERONA, ITALY

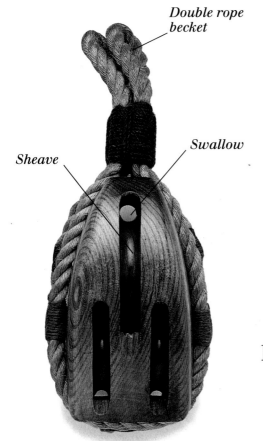

Double rope becket

Sheave

Swallow

DUTCH TRIPLE FIDDLE BLOCK

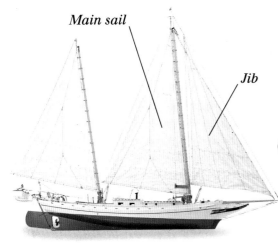

Main sail

Jib

CHESAPEAKE BAY BATEAU

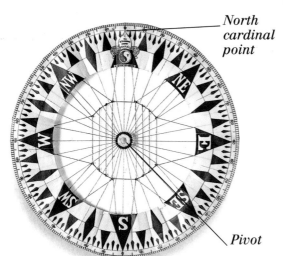

North cardinal point

Pivot

KELVIN LIGHT DRY COMPASS CARD

Contents

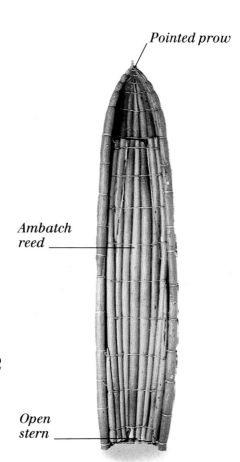

Pointed prow

Ambatch reed

Open stern

REED BOAT OF KENYA

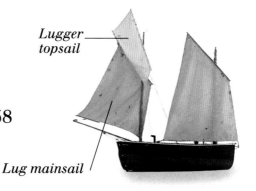

Lugger topsail

Lug mainsail

LUGGER

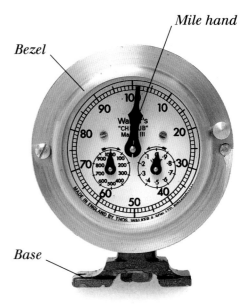

Mile hand

Bezel

Base

PATENT LOG REGISTER

The first boats

EARLY PEOPLE NEEDED BOATS TO TRAVEL, to trade and hunt, and to fish. They propelled their boats by hand, paddle, punting pole, or simple sail. Other than a floating tree trunk, man's first means of water transport was probably a raft. The Australian raft (right) could be built with the most elementary tools. Dugout logs and reeds—which are very light—were the materials most often used for early boats. The reed-built caballito was paddled through the surf of South American coastal waters, more like a float than a boat. The circular Iraqi guffa was used to carry cargo. It was simple to construct, and was often discarded once the journey was over. The guffa was made waterproof by being covered with pitch. By the third millenium B.C. the Egyptians were constructing sickle-shaped boats, like that at the bottom of the page, with cedar from Lebanon. The Egyptians also harnessed the wind with simple sails like that on the contemporary model of a traveling boat opposite. These boats were sailed from the Nile to trade with countries around the Mediterranean Sea.

WESTERN AUSTRALIAN RAFT

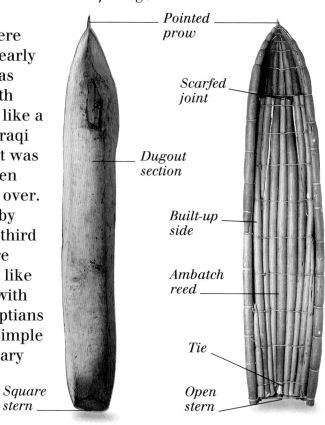

Wooden peg
Flat end
Shaped log
Pointed prow
Scarfed joint
Dugout section
Built-up side
Ambatch reed
Tie
Open stern
Square stern

HAITIAN DUGOUT CANOE
REED BOAT OF KENYA

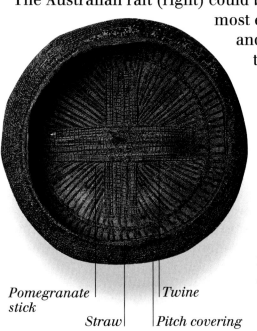

Pomegranate stick
Straw
Twine
Pitch covering

IRAQI GUFFA

PERUVIAN CABALLITO (COASTAL REED BOAT)

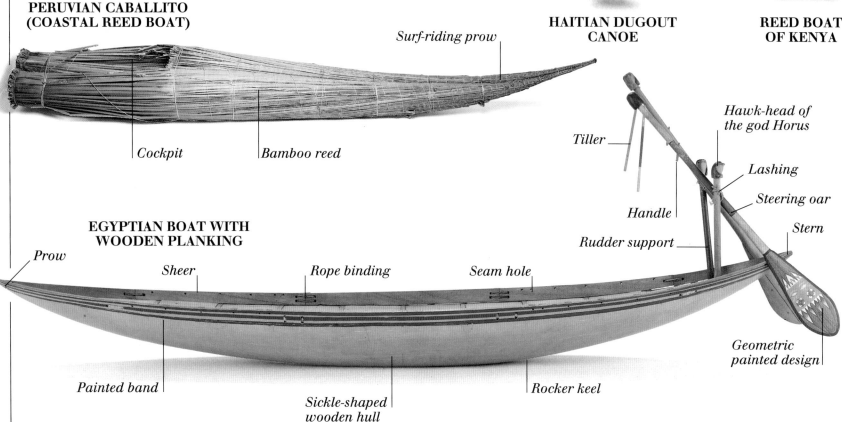

Surf-riding prow
Cockpit
Bamboo reed

Tiller
Hawk-head of the god Horus
Lashing
Steering oar
Handle
Stern
Rudder support
Geometric painted design

EGYPTIAN BOAT WITH WOODEN PLANKING

Prow
Sheer
Rope binding
Seam hole
Painted band
Sickle-shaped wooden hull
Rocker keel

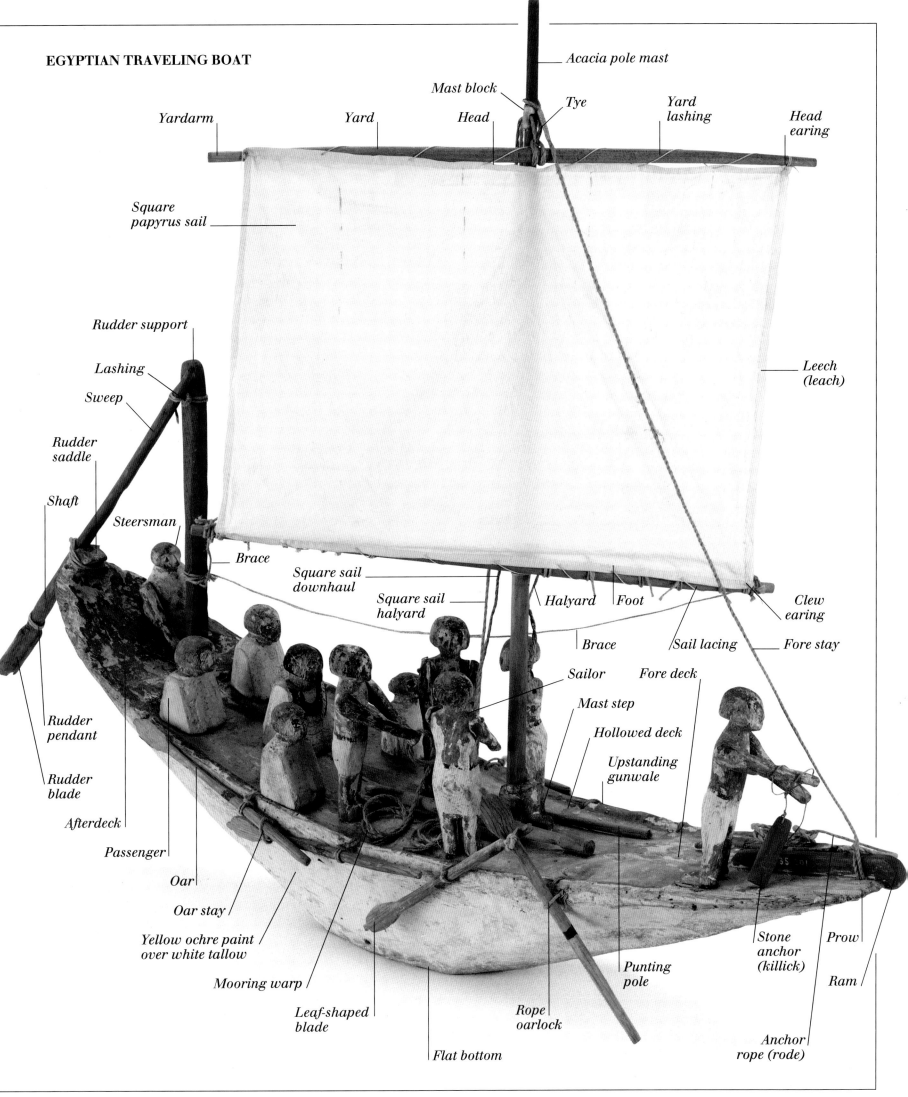

EGYPTIAN TRAVELING BOAT

Acacia pole mast

Mast block

Tye

Yardarm

Yard

Head

Yard lashing

Head earing

Square papyrus sail

Rudder support

Lashing

Leech (leach)

Sweep

Rudder saddle

Shaft

Steersman

Brace

Square sail downhaul

Square sail halyard

Halyard

Foot

Clew earing

Brace

Sail lacing

Fore stay

Rudder pendant

Rudder blade

Sailor

Fore deck

Mast step

Hollowed deck

Upstanding gunwale

Afterdeck

Passenger

Oar

Oar stay

Yellow ochre paint over white tallow

Mooring warp

Leaf-shaped blade

Rope oarlock

Stone anchor (killick)

Prow

Ram

Punting pole

Anchor rope (rode)

Flat bottom

Ships of Greece and Rome

ROMAN ANCHOR

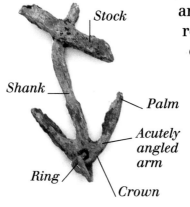

Stock

Shank

Palm

Acutely angled arm

Ring

Crown

IN THE EXPANSIVE EMPIRES OF GREECE AND ROME, powerful fleets were needed for battle, trade, and communication. Greek galleys were powered by a sail and many oars. A new armament, the embolos (ram), was fitted on to the galley bow. As ramming duels required fast and maneuverable boats, extra rows of oarsmen were added, culminating in the trireme. During the fifth and fourth centuries B.C., the trireme dominated the Mediterranean. It was powered by 170 oarsmen, each pulling one oar, and ranged on three levels, as the model opposite shows. The trireme also carried archers and soldiers for boarding enemy craft. Galleys were pulled out of the water when not in use, and were kept in dockyard ship-sheds. The merchant ships of the Greeks and Romans were mighty vessels, too. The full-bodied Roman corbita, for example, could hold up to 400 tons of cargo, such as spices, gems, silk, and animals. The construction of these boats was based on a stout hull with planking secured by mortice and tenon. Some of these ships made long trading voyages, sailing even as far as India. To make them easier to steer, corbitas set a foresail called an "artemon." It flew from a forward-leaning mast that was the forerunner of the long bowsprits carried by the great clipper ships of the 19th century.

ATTIC VASE SHOWING A GREEK GALLEY

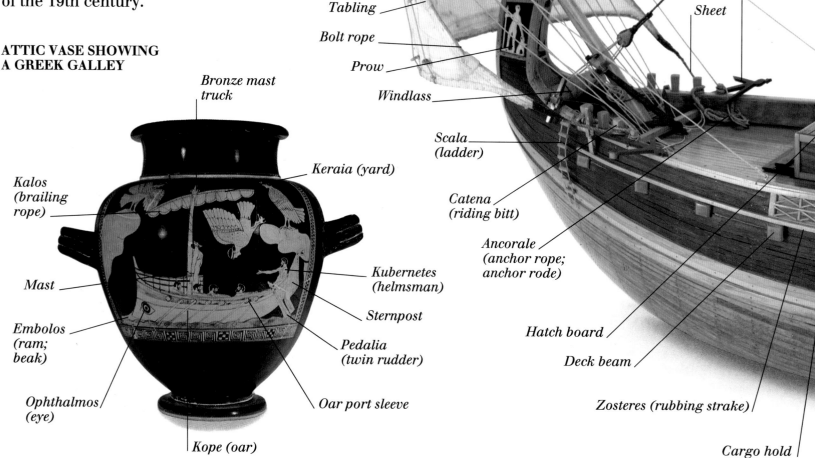

Bronze mast truck

Kalos (brailing rope)

Keraia (yard)

Mast

Embolos (ram; beak)

Kubernetes (helmsman)

Sternpost

Pedalia (twin rudder)

Ophthalmos (eye)

Oar port sleeve

Kope (oar)

ROMAN CORBITA

Double halyard

Roband (rope band)

Ceruchi (lift)

Bullseye

Heraldic device

Fore mast

Ring

Antenna (yard)

Buntline

Ruden (brail line)

Brace

Artemon (fore sail)

Fore stay

Oculus (eye)

Anchor

Tabling

Sheet

Bolt rope

Prow

Windlass

Scala (ladder)

Catena (riding bitt)

Ancorale (anchor rope; anchor rode)

Hatch board

Deck beam

Zosteres (rubbing strake)

Cargo hold

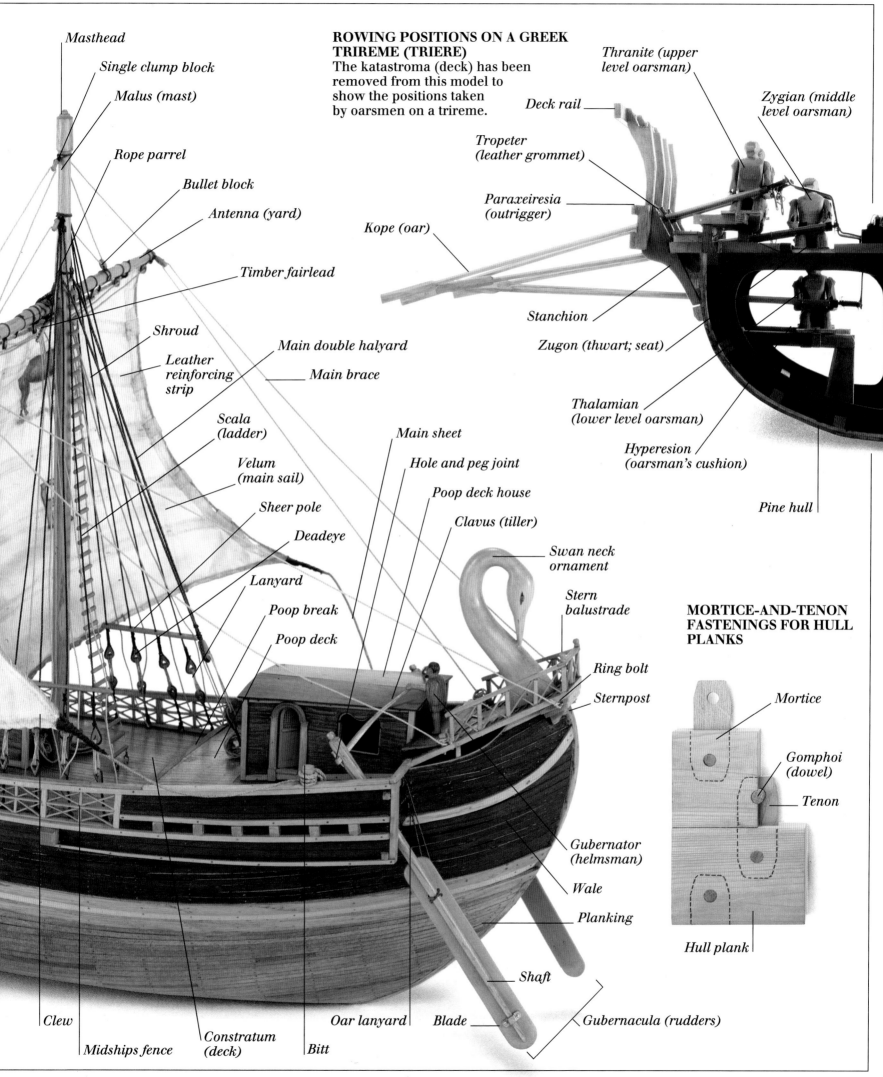

Masthead

Single clump block

Malus (mast)

Rope parrel

Bullet block

Antenna (yard)

Timber fairlead

Shroud

Leather
reinforcing
strip

Main double halyard

Main brace

Scala
(ladder)

Velum
(main sail)

Sheer pole

Deadeye

Lanyard

Poop break

Poop deck

Clew

Midships fence

Constratum
(deck)

Bitt

**ROWING POSITIONS ON A GREEK
TRIREME (TRIERE)**
The katastroma (deck) has been
removed from this model to
show the positions taken
by oarsmen on a trireme.

Thranite (upper
level oarsman)

Zygian (middle
level oarsman)

Deck rail

Tropeter
(leather grommet)

Paraxeiresia
(outrigger)

Kope (oar)

Stanchion

Zugon (thwart; seat)

Thalamian
(lower level oarsman)

Hyperesion
(oarsman's cushion)

Pine hull

Main sheet

Hole and peg joint

Poop deck house

Clavus (tiller)

Swan neck
ornament

Stern
balustrade

Ring bolt

Sternpost

Gubernator
(helmsman)

Wale

Planking

Shaft

Oar lanyard

Blade

Gubernacula (rudders)

**MORTICE-AND-TENON
FASTENINGS FOR HULL
PLANKS**

Mortice

Gomphoi
(dowel)

Tenon

Hull plank

Viking ships

IN THE DARK AGES (roughly 500 A.D. to 1000 A.D.) the longships of Scandinavia were among the most feared sights for people of northern Europe. The Vikings launched raids from Scandinavia every summer in longships equipped with a single steering oar on the right, or "steerboard" side (hence, "starboard"). A longboat had one row of oars on each side and a single sail. The hull was clinker-built, with overlapping planks. Prowheads adorned fighting ships during war campaigns. The longship was also used for coastal travel. The karv below was probably built as transport for an important family, while the smaller faering was a rowing boat only. The fleet of William of Normandy that invaded England in 1066 owed much to the Viking boat building tradition, and has been depicted in the Bayeux Tapestry (right). Seals of port towns and royal courts through the ages provide a record of contemporary ship design. The seal opposite shows a European craft from somewhat later than the Viking period. Fighting platforms, or castles, and the addition of more masts and sails changed the character of the medieval ship. Note also that the steering oar has been replaced by a centered rudder.

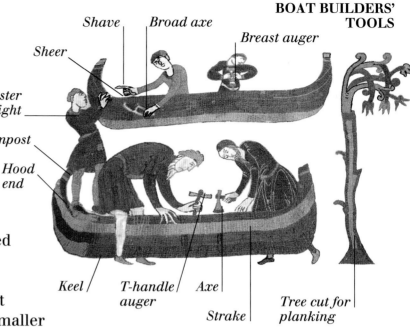

BOAT BUILDERS' TOOLS

Shave
Broad axe
Breast auger
Sheer
Master shipwright
Stempost
Hood end
Keel
T-handle auger
Axe
Strake
Tree cut for planking

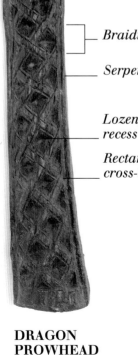

Zoomorphic head

Eye

Tooth

Braiding

Serpentine neck

Lozenge-shaped recess

Rectangular cross-band

DRAGON PROWHEAD

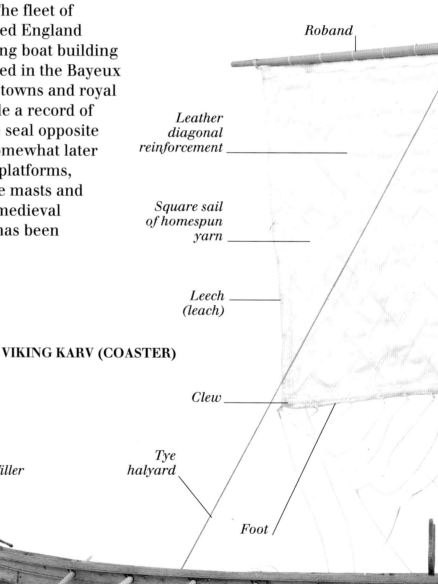

Roband

Leather diagonal reinforcement

Square sail of homespun yarn

Leech (leach)

Clew

Tye halyard

Foot

Snake-tail ornament

VIKING KARV (COASTER)

Sternpost

Boss (rudder pivot)

Tiller

Steering oar (side rudder)

Oar

Starboard (steerboard) side

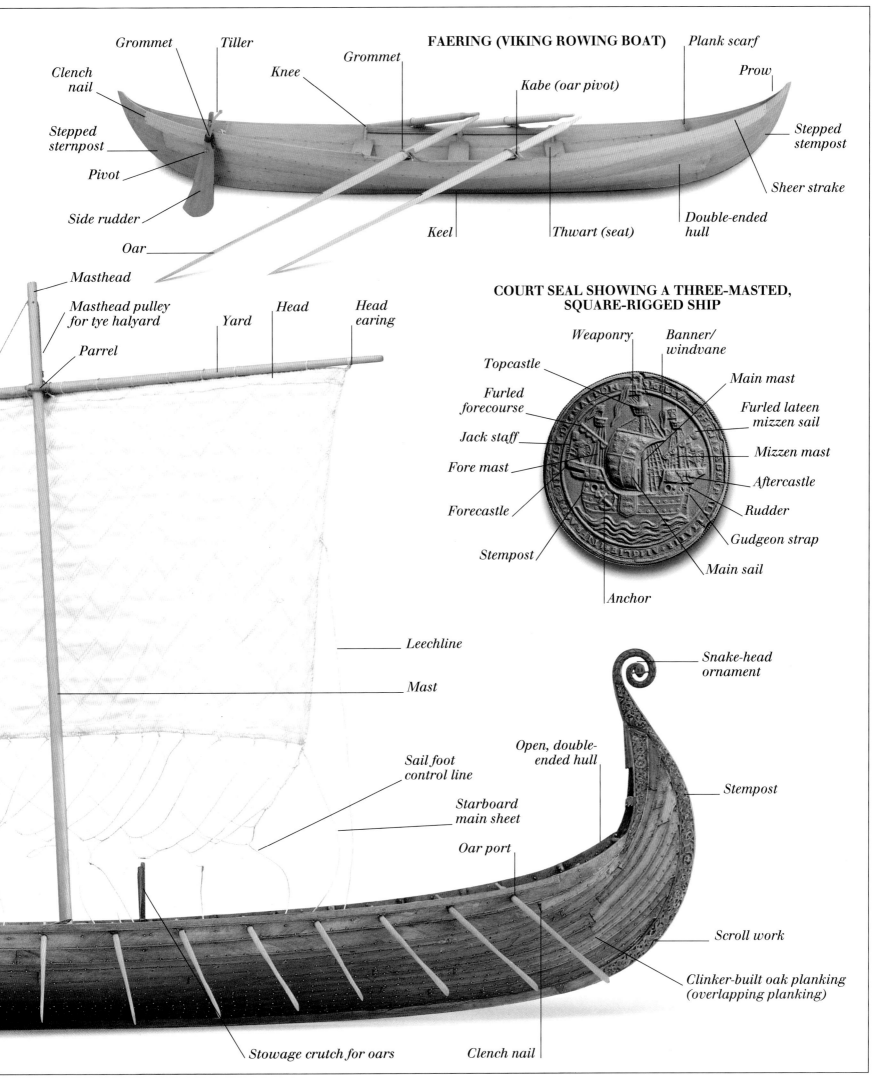

FAERING (VIKING ROWING BOAT)

Grommet

Tiller

Clench nail

Grommet

Knee

Kabe (oar pivot)

Plank scarf

Prow

Stepped sternpost

Stepped stempost

Pivot

Side rudder

Sheer strake

Oar

Keel

Thwart (seat)

Double-ended hull

Masthead

Masthead pulley for tye halyard

Yard

Head

Head earing

COURT SEAL SHOWING A THREE-MASTED, SQUARE-RIGGED SHIP

Parrel

Weaponry

Banner/ windvane

Topcastle

Main mast

Furled forecourse

Furled lateen mizzen sail

Jack staff

Mizzen mast

Fore mast

Aftercastle

Forecastle

Rudder

Stempost

Gudgeon strap

Main sail

Anchor

Leechline

Snake-head ornament

Mast

Sail foot control line

Open, double-ended hull

Stempost

Starboard main sheet

Oar port

Scroll work

Clinker-built oak planking (overlapping planking)

Stowage crutch for oars

Clench nail

11

Ships for war and trade

FROM THE 16TH CENTURY, SHIPS WERE BUILT WITH A NEW FORM OF HULL, constructed with carvel (edge-to-edge) planking. Warships of the time, like King Henry VIII of England's Mary Rose, boasted awesome fire power. This ship carried both long-range bronze cannon, and short-range, anti personnel guns in iron. Elsewhere, ships took on a multiformity of shapes. Dhows transported slaves from East Africa to Arabia, their fore-and-aft rigged lateen sails allowing them to sail close to the wind around the lands of the Indian Ocean. The Chinese sailed to East Africa and Arabia in junks, trading goods that were carried in watertight compartments. New astronomical tools helped medieval sailors to find their way. Cross-staves and astrolabes were used to measure the altitude of the sun or stars. One of the cross-pieces was slid along the staff of the cross-stave—which was graduated in degrees of altitude—until its top aligned with the celestial body and its base with the horizon. The sighting rule of the astrolabe was simply lined up with a known body, and its altitude read from marks on the metal disk. Sundials used the shadow of the sun to show sailors the time of day.

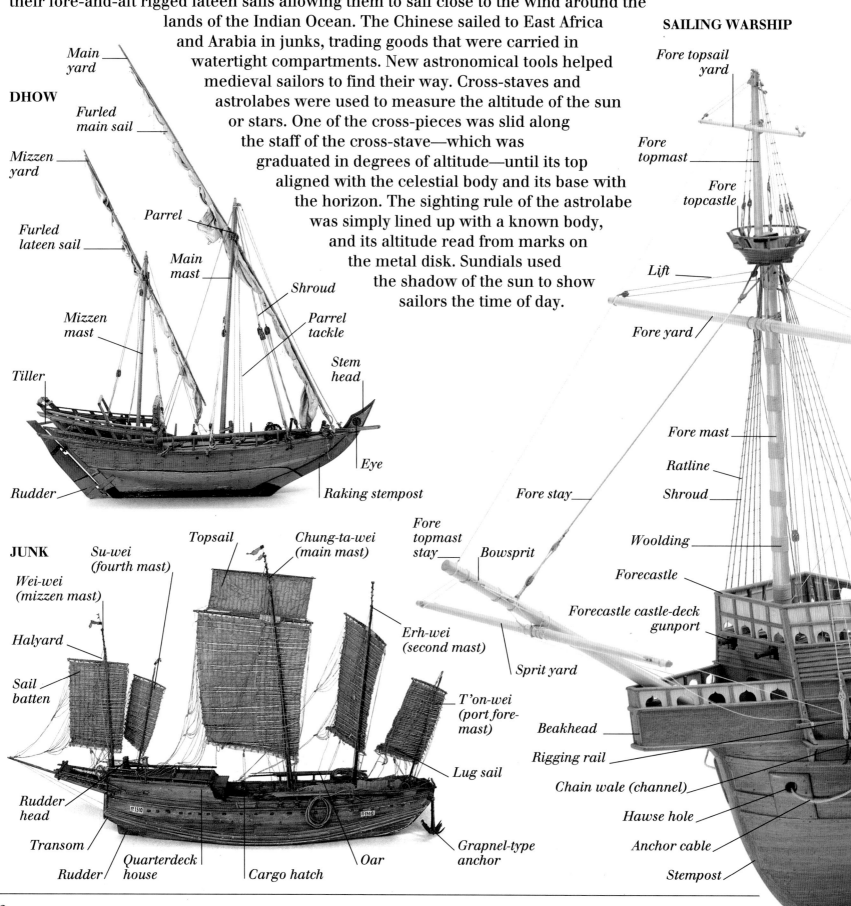

SAILING WARSHIP

Fore topsail yard

Fore topmast

Fore topcastle

Lift

Fore yard

Fore mast

Ratline

Shroud

Fore stay

Woolding

Fore topmast stay

Bowsprit

Forecastle

Forecastle castle-deck gunport

Sprit yard

Beakhead

Rigging rail

Chain wale (channel)

Hawse hole

Anchor cable

Stempost

DHOW

Main yard

Furled main sail

Mizzen yard

Parrel

Furled lateen sail

Main mast

Mizzen mast

Shroud

Parrel tackle

Stem head

Tiller

Rudder

Eye

Raking stempost

JUNK

Su-wei (fourth mast)

Wei-wei (mizzen mast)

Topsail

Chung-ta-wei (main mast)

Halyard

Erh-wei (second mast)

Sail batten

T'on-wei (port fore-mast)

Lug sail

Rudder head

Transom

Rudder

Quarterdeck house

Oar

Cargo hatch

Grapnel-type anchor

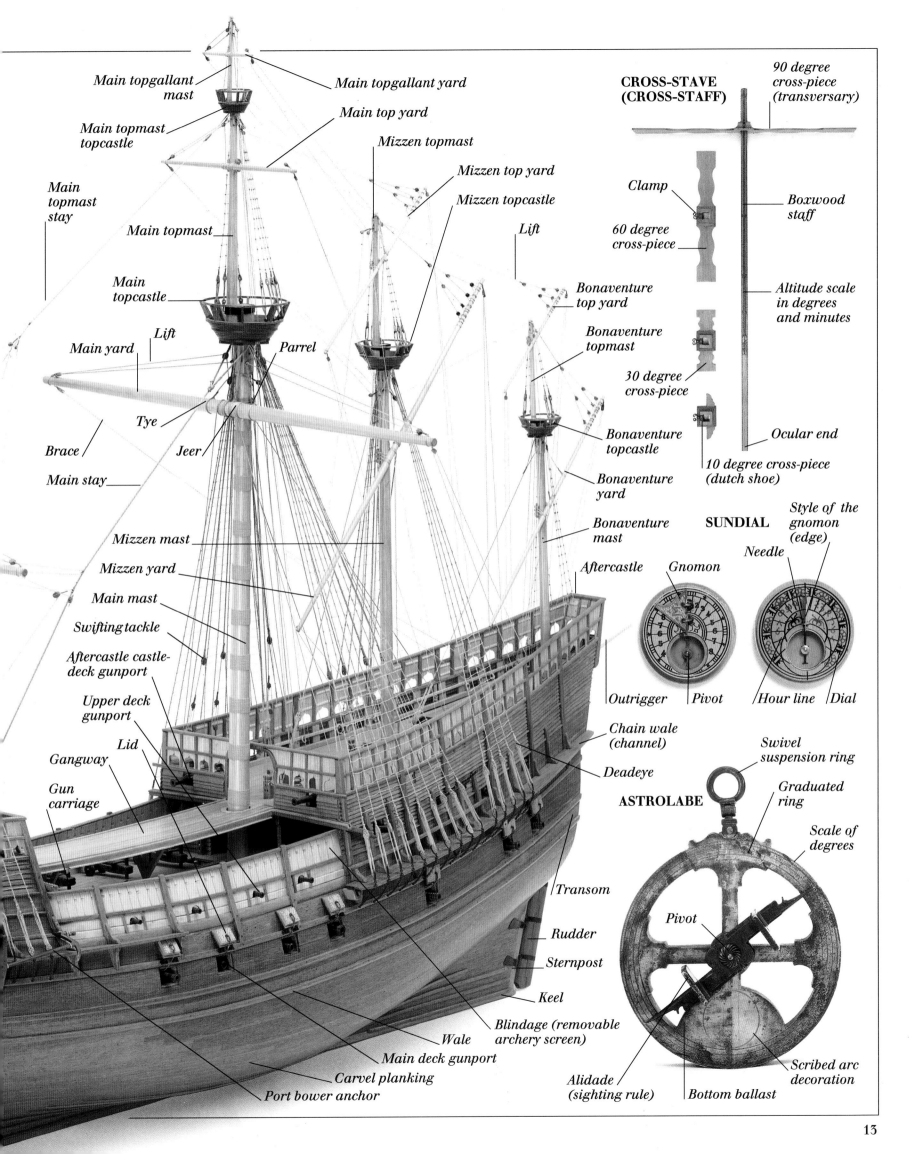

Main topgallant mast

Main topgallant yard

Main topmast topcastle

Main top yard

Mizzen topmast

Mizzen top yard

Main topmast stay

Mizzen topcastle

Main topmast

Lift

Main topcastle

Bonaventure top yard

Lift

Main yard

Lift

Parrel

Bonaventure topmast

Main yard

Tye

30 degree cross-piece

Brace

Jeer

Bonaventure topcastle

Main stay

Bonaventure yard

Bonaventure mast

Mizzen mast

Aftercastle

Mizzen yard

Main mast

Swifting tackle

Aftercastle castle-deck gunport

Upper deck gunport

Lid

Gangway

Gun carriage

Chain wale (channel)

Deadeye

Transom

Rudder

Sternpost

Keel

Blindage (removable archery screen)

Wale

Main deck gunport

Carvel planking

Port bower anchor

CROSS-STAVE (CROSS-STAFF)

90 degree cross-piece (transversary)

Clamp

Boxwood staff

60 degree cross-piece

Altitude scale in degrees and minutes

Ocular end

10 degree cross-piece (dutch shoe)

SUNDIAL

Style of the gnomon (edge)

Needle

Gnomon

Outrigger   Pivot

Hour line   Dial

ASTROLABE

Swivel suspension ring

Graduated ring

Scale of degrees

Pivot

Alidade (sighting rule)

Bottom ballast

Scribed arc decoration

The expansion of sail

By the 18th century, sailing ships had become fast and effective floating fortresses. The navies of the north European powers competed with each other by building heavily-armed fighting ships called "men-of-war." The distinctive round stern of the ship below, with its open gallery, balcony, and elaborate wood carving is typical of the period. Hulls around this time were semicircular in cross section, although many boat designers were soon to return to the V-shaped hulls used by the Vikings. Ships of the period carried more sail than ever before. A labyrinth of rigging supported the masts and yards from which the profusion of square sails were set. Ships grew higher as extra masts were fitted above the lower masts, and the bowsprit became longer, to allow the ship to carry staysails, spritsails, and jibs. Ships went into battle in single file, so that broadsides from the multiple decks of guns would have maximum effect. Ships were classified by rates, the rating of a vessel depending on how many guns it had. A first rate ship had more than 100 guns. The guns fired solid round shot, usually made of iron.

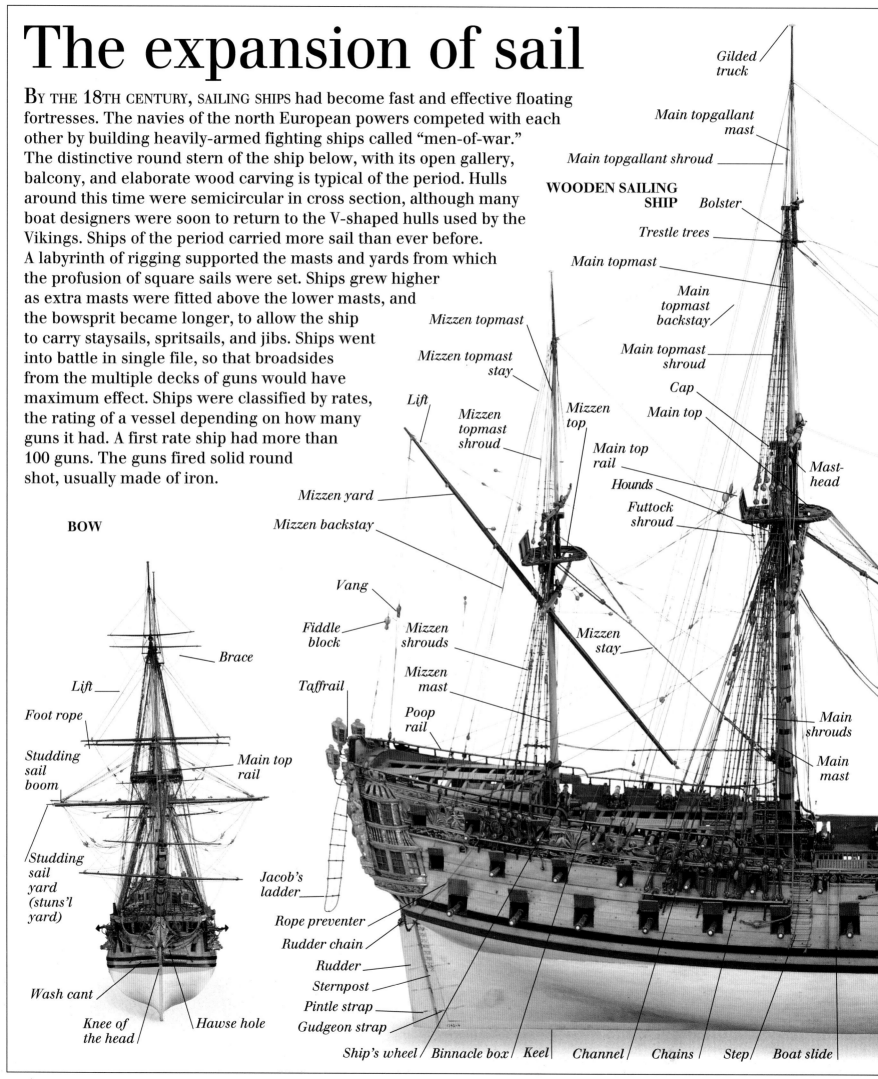

WOODEN SAILING SHIP

Gilded truck

Main topgallant mast

Main topgallant shroud

Bolster

Trestle trees

Main topmast

Main topmast backstay

Mizzen topmast

Main topmast shroud

Mizzen topmast stay

Cap

Lift

Mizzen topmast shroud

Mizzen top

Main top

Main top rail

Hounds

Masthead

Mizzen yard

Futtock shroud

Mizzen backstay

Main top rail

Vang

Fiddle block

Mizzen shrouds

Mizzen stay

Taffrail

Mizzen mast

Poop rail

Main shrouds

Main mast

BOW

Brace

Lift

Foot rope

Studding sail boom

Main top rail

Studding sail yard (stuns'l yard)

Jacob's ladder

Rope preventer

Rudder chain

Rudder

Sternpost

Pintle strap

Gudgeon strap

Wash cant

Knee of the head

Hawse hole

Ship's wheel   Binnacle box   Keel   Channel   Chains   Step   Boat slide

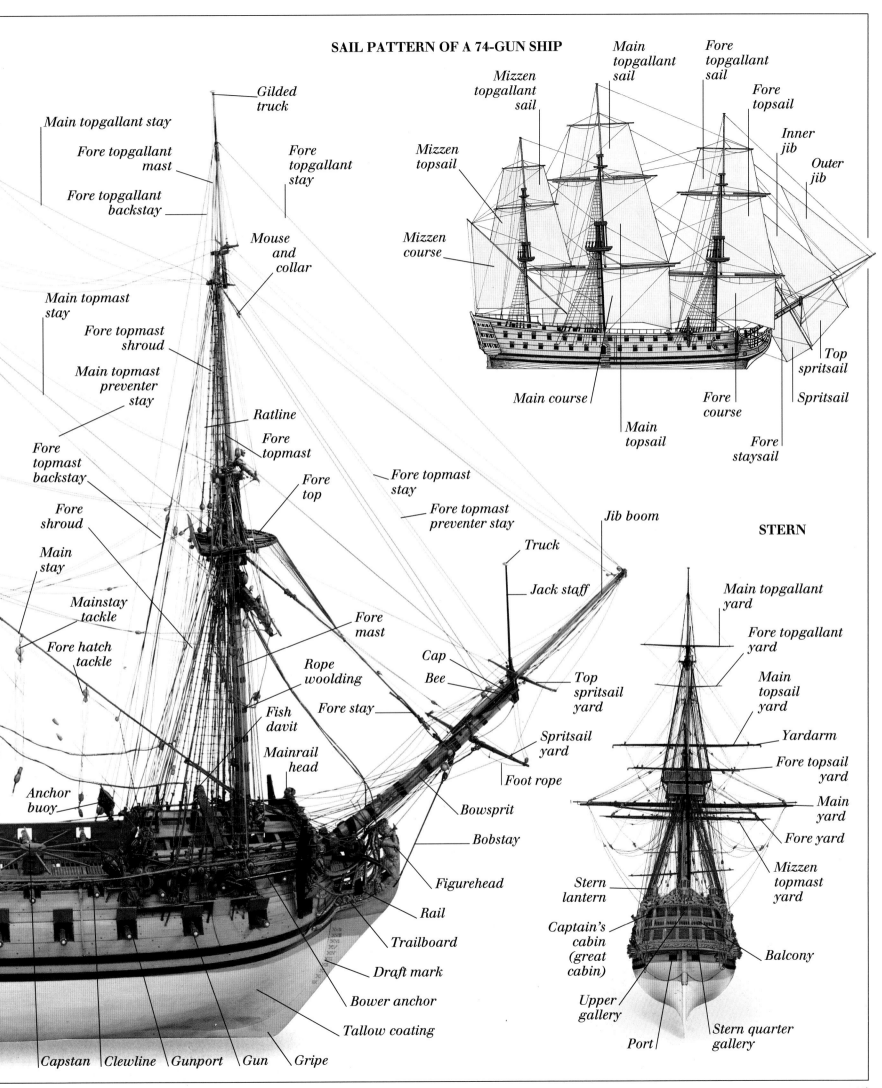

SAIL PATTERN OF A 74-GUN SHIP

Main topgallant stay

Fore topgallant mast

Fore topgallant backstay

Gilded truck

Fore topgallant stay

Mouse and collar

Main topmast stay

Fore topmast shroud

Main topmast preventer stay

Ratline

Fore topmast

Fore top

Fore topmast stay

Fore topmast preventer stay

Fore topmast backstay

Fore shroud

Main stay

Mainstay tackle

Fore hatch tackle

Anchor buoy

Fore mast

Rope woolding

Fore stay

Fish davit

Mainrail head

Jib boom

Truck

Jack staff

Cap

Bee

Top spritsail yard

Spritsail yard

Foot rope

Bowsprit

Bobstay

Figurehead

Rail

Trailboard

Draft mark

Bower anchor

Tallow coating

Capstan | Clewline | Gunport | Gun | Gripe

Mizzen topgallant sail

Main topgallant sail

Fore topgallant sail

Fore topsail

Mizzen topsail

Mizzen course

Inner jib

Outer jib

Main course

Main topsail

Fore course

Fore staysail

Top spritsail

Spritsail

STERN

Main topgallant yard

Fore topgallant yard

Main topsail yard

Yardarm

Fore topsail yard

Main yard

Fore yard

Mizzen topmast yard

Stern lantern

Captain's cabin (great cabin)

Balcony

Upper gallery

Port

Stern quarter gallery

15

A ship of the line

T<small>HE</small> 74-<small>GUN</small> <small>THIRD-RATER WAS A MAINSTAY</small> of British and French battlefleets in the late 18th and early 19th centuries. (The biggest ships in the fledgling American navy of the time were 44-gun frigates.) The length of such a man-of-war was determined by the number of guns needed for each deck, allowing room for crews to man them. The gun deck of this vessel was about 170 ft (52 m) long. Her decks had to be strong to carry the weight of the guns. The deck planks have been removed in the model below to illustrate the number of beams needed to make the hull strong enough. Only timber with perfect grain was used. The upper deck was open at the waist, but forward and aft were officers' cabins. The forecastle (foc's'l) and quarterdeck carried light guns and provided platforms for handling the rigging and for reconnaissance. The ship's longboats, or launches, were carried on skids between the gangways.

UPPER DECK OF A 74-GUN SHIP

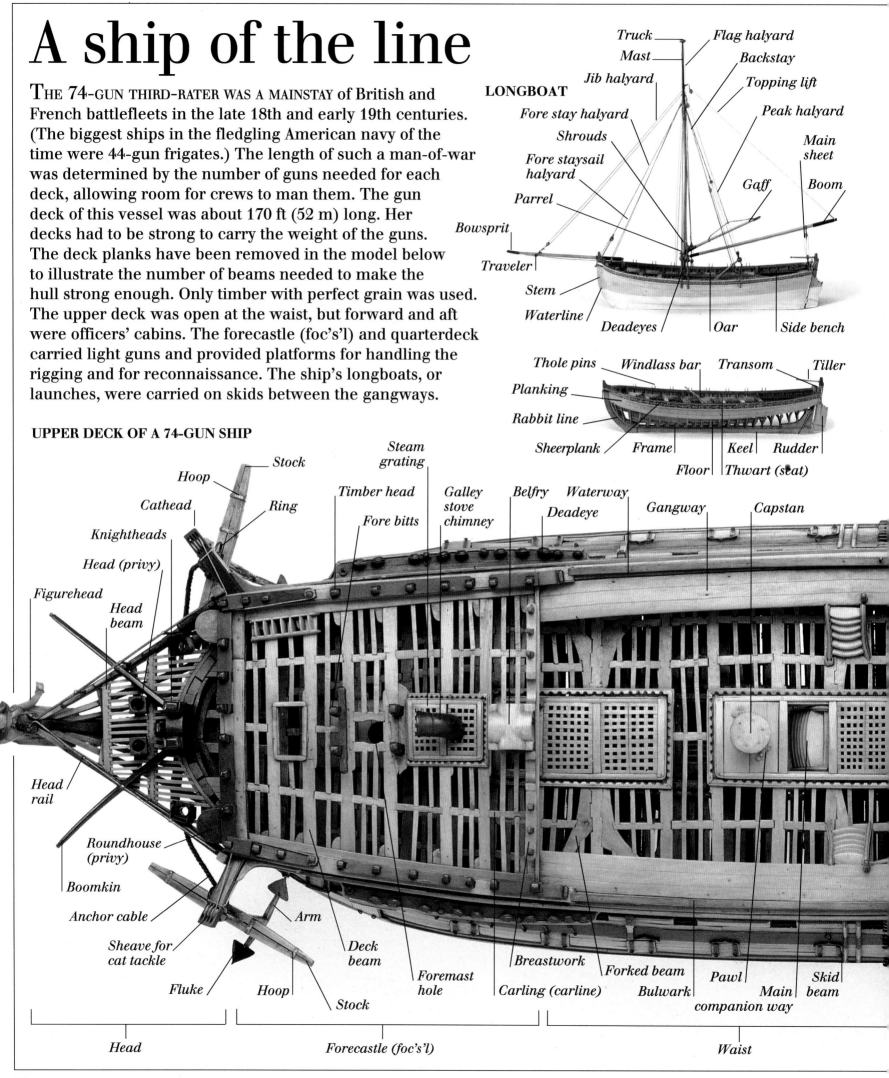

LONGBOAT

Truck • Flag halyard
Mast • Backstay
Jib halyard • Topping lift
Fore stay halyard • Peak halyard
Shrouds • Main sheet
Fore staysail halyard
Parrel • Gaff • Boom
Bowsprit
Traveler
Stem
Waterline • Deadeyes • Oar • Side bench

Thole pins • Windlass bar • Transom • Tiller
Planking
Rabbit line • Sheerplank • Frame • Keel • Rudder
Floor • Thwart (seat)

Stock
Hoop • Steam grating
Cathead • Ring
Knightheads • Timber head • Galley stove chimney • Belfry • Waterway
Head (privy) • Fore bitts • Deadeye • Gangway • Capstan
Figurehead
Head beam
Head rail
Roundhouse (privy)
Boomkin
Anchor cable • Arm
Sheave for cat tackle
Fluke • Hoop • Deck beam • Foremast hole
Stock
Breastwork • Forked beam • Pawl • Skid beam
Carling (carline) • Bulwark • Main companion way

Head
Forecastle (foc's'l)
Waist

16

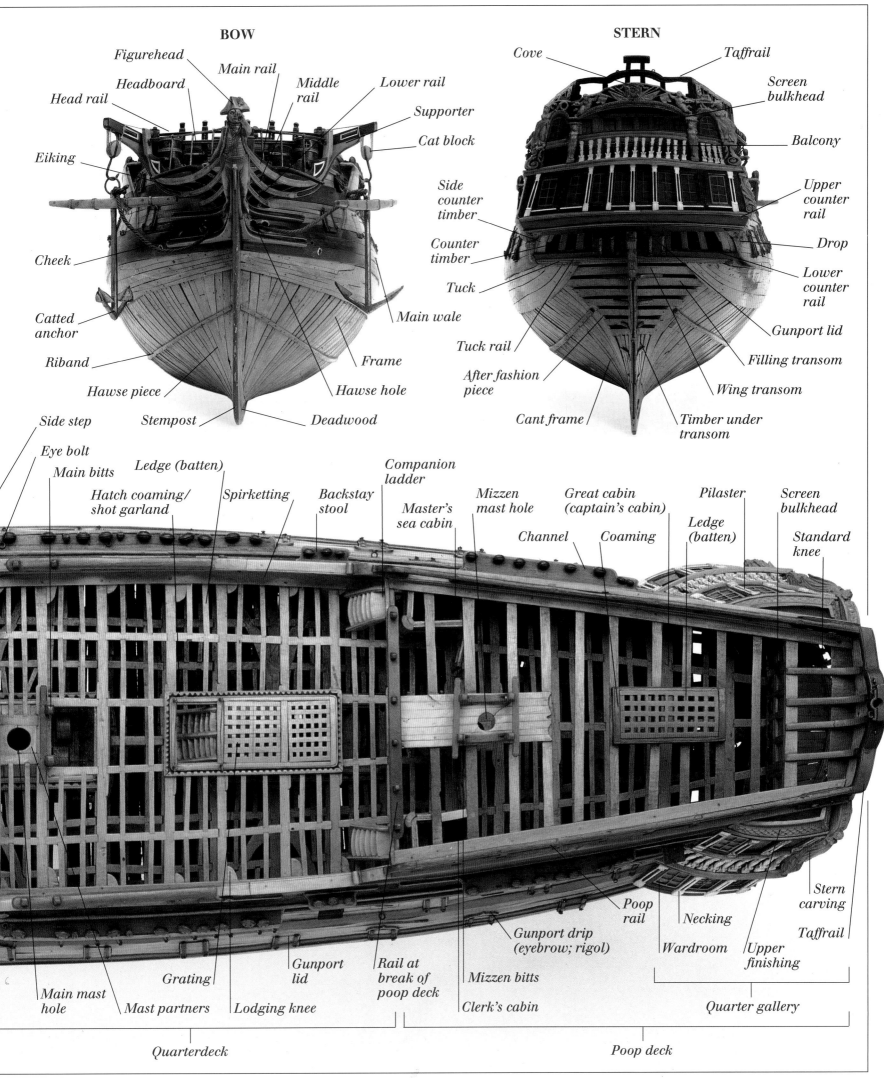

BOW

Figurehead

Headboard

Head rail

Main rail

Middle rail

Lower rail

Supporter

Cat block

Eiking

Cheek

Catted anchor

Riband

Side step

Eye bolt

Main bitts

Hatch coaming/ shot garland

Ledge (batten)

Spirketting

Backstay stool

Master's sea cabin

Companion ladder

Mizzen mast hole

Great cabin (captain's cabin)

Channel

Coaming

Pilaster

Ledge (batten)

Screen bulkhead

Standard knee

Hawse piece

Stempost

Deadwood

Main wale

Frame

Hawse hole

STERN

Cove

Taffrail

Screen bulkhead

Balcony

Upper counter rail

Drop

Side counter timber

Counter timber

Tuck

Tuck rail

After fashion piece

Cant frame

Lower counter rail

Gunport lid

Filling transom

Wing transom

Timber under transom

Main mast hole

Mast partners

Grating

Lodging knee

Gunport lid

Rail at break of poop deck

Gunport drip (eyebrow; rigol)

Mizzen bitts

Clerk's cabin

Poop rail

Necking

Wardroom

Upper finishing

Quarter gallery

Stern carving

Taffrail

Quarterdeck

Poop deck

Anatomy of a wooden ship

THE SKELETON OF A WOODEN SHIP is a complex system of timbers joined together to form the frame, on which the planks and decks are attached. The many parts of a man-of-war's frame are laid out flat below to show the shape of each unit. (The old-fashioned terms for each piece of the frame are given.) The completed frame of a smaller craft, a collier brig, is shown opposite. Ship builders used wood from specially grown trees called "grown oaks" (right), whose limbs conformed naturally to the shapes needed for the knees, ryders, and other pieces that make up the frame. Water and heat were used to bend the oak to the final fit.

GROWN OAKS (COMPASS TIMBERS)

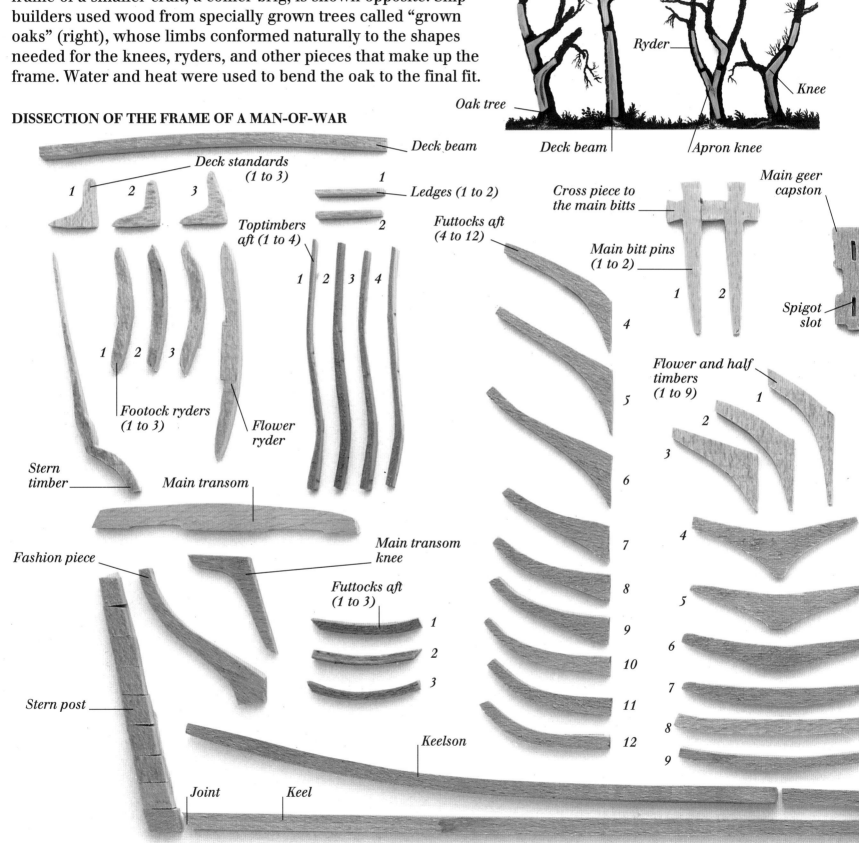

Ryder

Oak tree

Deck beam

Apron knee

Knee

DISSECTION OF THE FRAME OF A MAN-OF-WAR

Deck beam

Deck standards (1 to 3)

1   2   3

Ledges (1 to 2)

1

2

Toptimbers aft (1 to 4)

1   2   3   4

Footock ryders (1 to 3)

1   2   3

Flower ryder

Stern timber

Main transom

Main transom knee

Fashion piece

Futtocks aft (1 to 3)

1

2

3

Stern post

Joint   Keel

Keelson

Futtocks aft (4 to 12)

4

5

6

7

8

9

10

11

12

Cross piece to the main bitts

Main bitt pins (1 to 2)

1   2

Main geer capston

Spigot slot

Flower and half timbers (1 to 9)

1

2

3

4

5

6

7

8

9

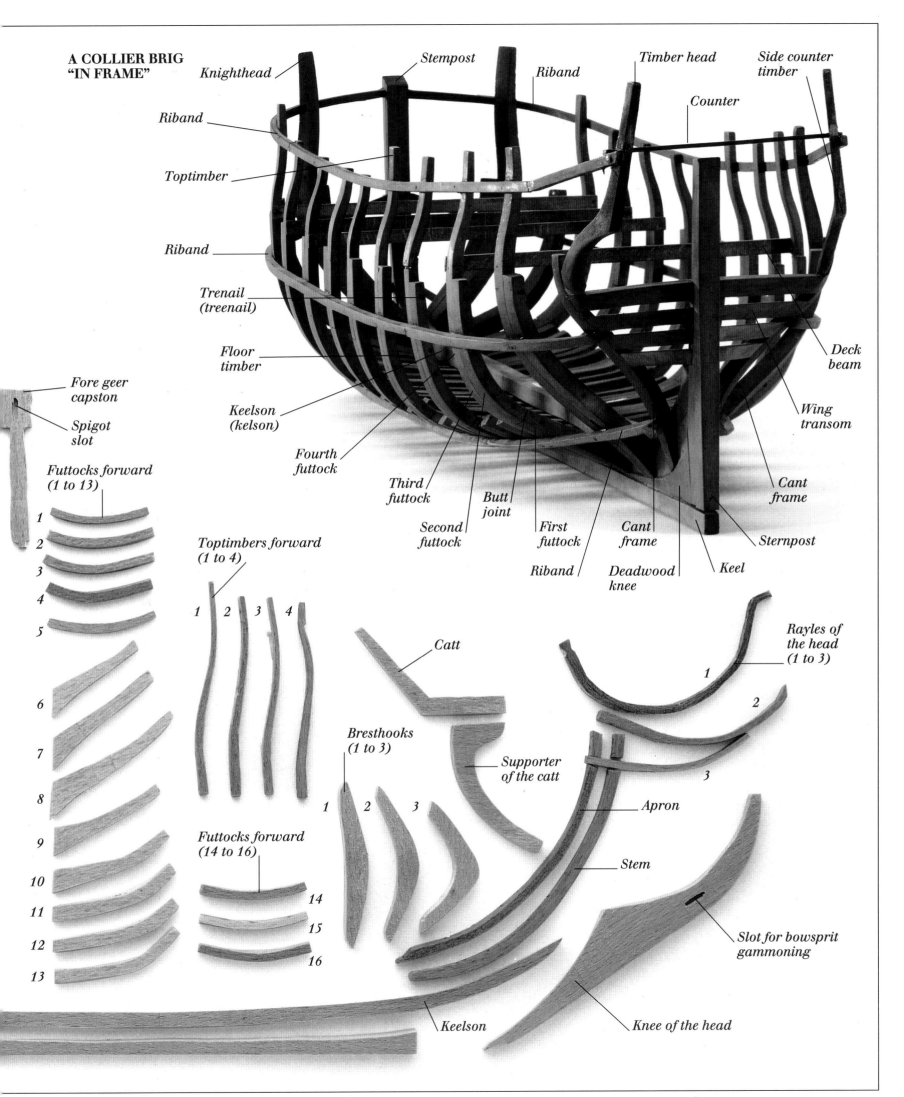

A COLLIER BRIG "IN FRAME"

Knighthead

Stempost

Riband

Timber head

Side counter timber

Riband

Counter

Toptimber

Riband

Trenail (treenail)

Floor timber

Deck beam

Keelson (kelson)

Wing transom

Fourth futtock

Third futtock

Butt joint

Second futtock

First futtock

Cant frame

Cant frame

Sternpost

Riband

Deadwood knee

Keel

Fore geer capston

Spigot slot

Futtocks forward (1 to 13)

1
2
3
4
5
6
7
8
9
10
11
12
13

Toptimbers forward (1 to 4)

1 2 3 4

Catt

Bresthooks (1 to 3)

1 2 3

Supporter of the catt

Rayles of the head (1 to 3)

1

2

3

Apron

Stem

Slot for bowsprit gammoning

Futtocks forward (14 to 16)

14
15
16

Keelson

Knee of the head

19

Anatomy of an iron ship

IRON PARTS WERE USED IN WOODEN SHIPS AS EARLY AS 1675, often in the same form as the wooden parts that they replaced. Eventually, as on the tea clipper Cutty Sark (below), iron standing rigging was found to be stronger than the traditional rope. The first "ironclads" were warships whose wooden hulls were protected by iron armor plates. Later ironclads actually had iron hulls. The model opposite is based on the British warship HMS Warrior, launched in 1860, the first battleship built entirely of iron. The plan of an iron paddlesteamer (bottom), built somewhat later, shows that the craft had the masts and bowsprit of a sailing ship; but it also boasted a steam propulsion plant amidships that turned two side paddlewheels. Early iron plates were painstakingly riveted together (below), but by the 1940s, steel vessels were welded together, whole sections at a time. The Liberty ships built in America during World War II are prime examples of such "production-line" vessels.

TEA CLIPPER

Steel yard

Iron wire stay

Steel lower mast

Steel bowsprit

Forged iron anchor

Wooden planking with copper sheathing

RIVETED PLATES

Pan head rivet

Plate

Button head rivet (snap head)

Seam

LIBERTY SHIP

Accommodation section

Cargo derrick

Weld line

Gun section

Stern section

Midships section

Cargo hold

Bow section

PLAN OF AN IRON PADDLESTEAMER

Mizzen mast

Poop deck

Lounge

Deck lantern

Main mast

Steam whistle

Crankshaft

Paddle wheel

Steering position

Guardrail

Binnacle

State room

After funnel

Guardrail

Eccentric

Connecting rod

Steering gear

Skylight

Stern

Vertical frame ladder

Mast step

Rudder

Rudder post

Heel of rudder post

Bar keel

Afterpeak

Tank

Main mast step

Box boiler

Reversing wheel

Side lever

Stern framing

Cabin

Donkey boiler

Foundation

Bottom plate

Cylinder

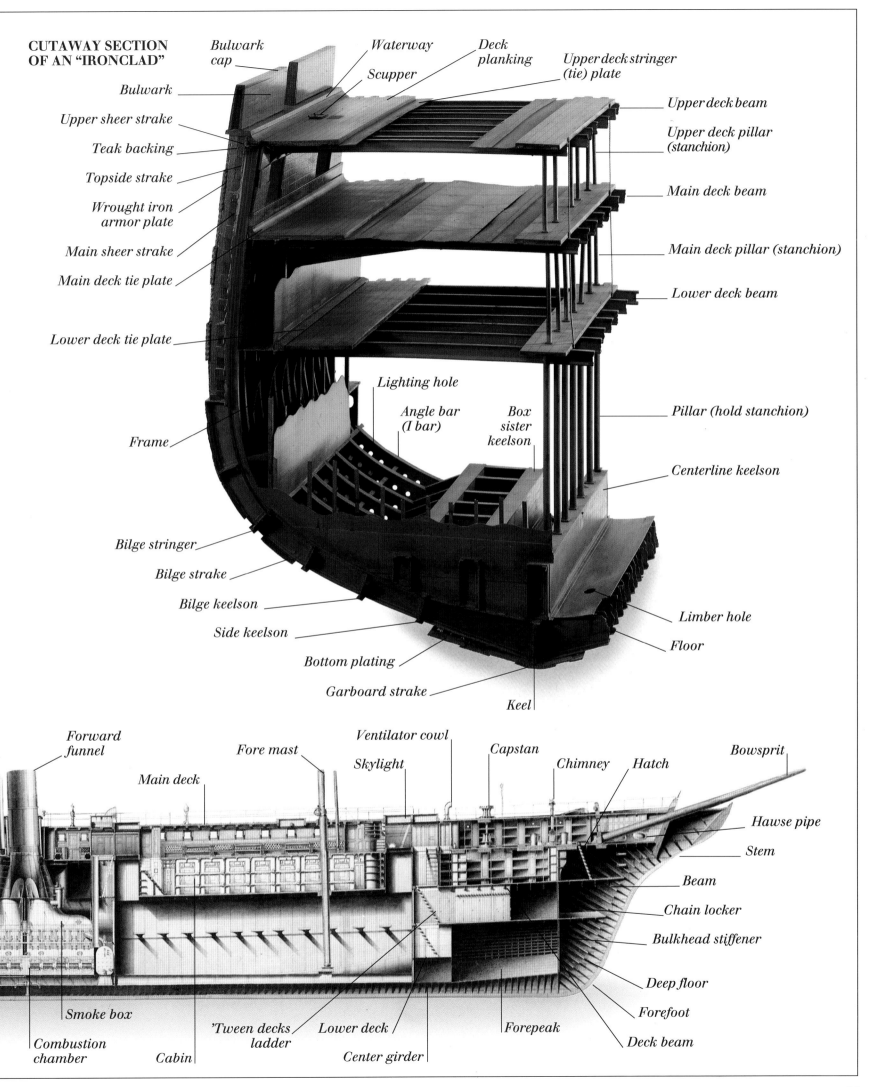

CUTAWAY SECTION OF AN "IRONCLAD"

Bulwark cap

Waterway

Scupper

Deck planking

Upper deck stringer (tie) plate

Bulwark

Upper sheer strake

Teak backing

Topside strake

Wrought iron armor plate

Main sheer strake

Main deck tie plate

Lower deck tie plate

Frame

Lighting hole

Angle bar (I bar)

Box sister keelson

Bilge stringer

Bilge strake

Bilge keelson

Side keelson

Bottom plating

Garboard strake

Keel

Upper deck beam

Upper deck pillar (stanchion)

Main deck beam

Main deck pillar (stanchion)

Lower deck beam

Pillar (hold stanchion)

Centerline keelson

Limber hole

Floor

Forward funnel

Ventilator cowl

Capstan

Bowsprit

Fore mast

Skylight

Chimney

Hatch

Main deck

Hawse pipe

Stem

Beam

Chain locker

Bulkhead stiffener

Deep floor

Forefoot

Smoke box

'Tween decks ladder

Lower deck

Forepeak

Deck beam

Combustion chamber

Cabin

Center girder

Paddle wheels and propellers

THE INVENTION OF THE STEAM ENGINE IN THE 18TH CENTURY made mechanically driven ships fitted with paddle wheels or propellers a viable alternative to sails. Paddle wheels have fixed or feathered floats, and the model shown below features both types. Feathered floats give more propulsive power than fixed floats because they are almost upright at all times in the water. Paddle wheels were superseded by the propeller on oceangoing vessels in the mid-19th century. Propellers are more efficient, work better in rough water, and are less vulnerable in collisions. The first propellers were two-bladed, but later three- and four-bladed versions are more powerful; the shape and pitch of the blades have also been refined over the years. At the beginning of the 18th century, tillers were replaced on many larger ships by the ship's wheel as a means of steering.

SHIP'S WHEEL

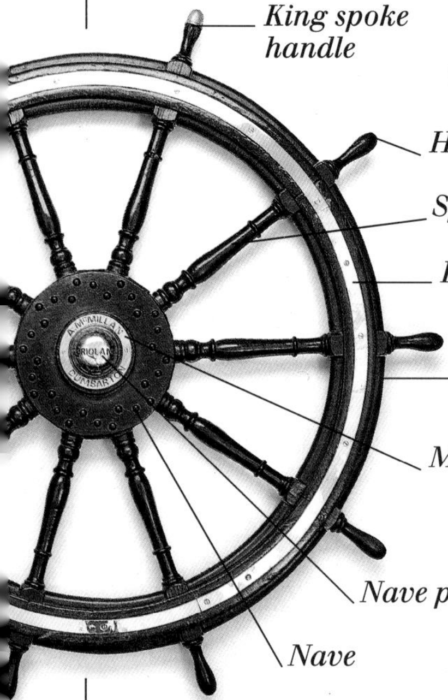

King spoke handle

Handle

Spoke

Rim plate

Felloe (rim section)

Maker's name

Nave plate

Nave

PADDLE WHEEL WITH FIXED FLOATS

Wrist pin

Limb

Fixed float

Hub

Deck beam

OSCILLATING STEAM ENGINE

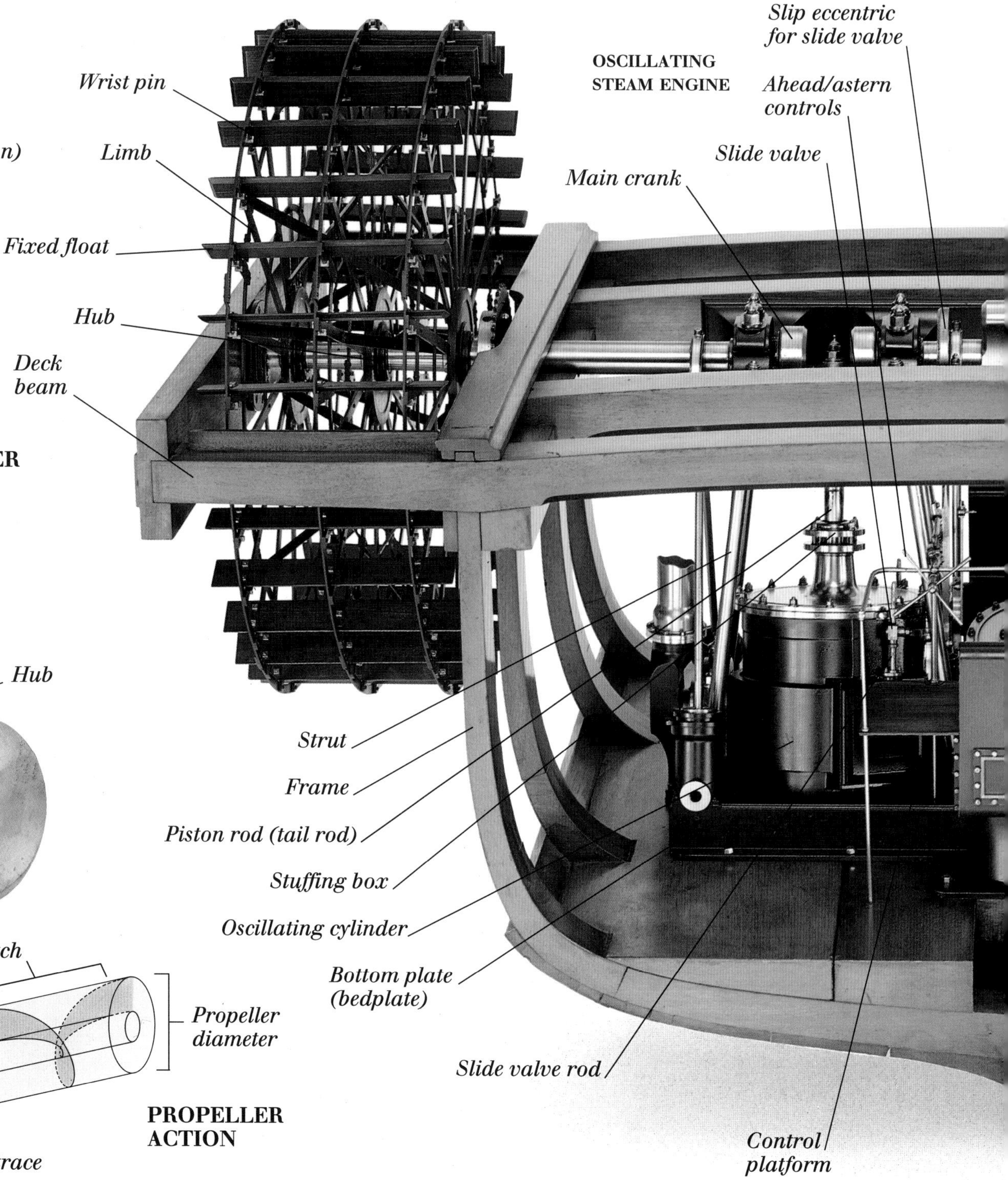

Slip eccentric for slide valve

Ahead/astern controls

Slide valve

Main crank

THREE-BLADED PROPELLER

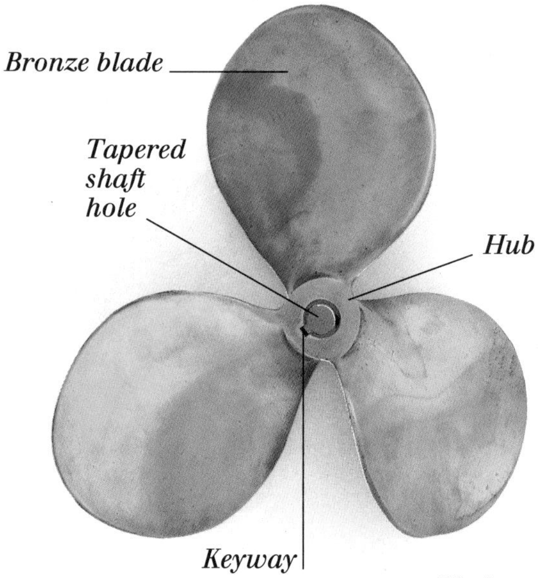

Bronze blade

Tapered shaft hole

Hub

Keyway

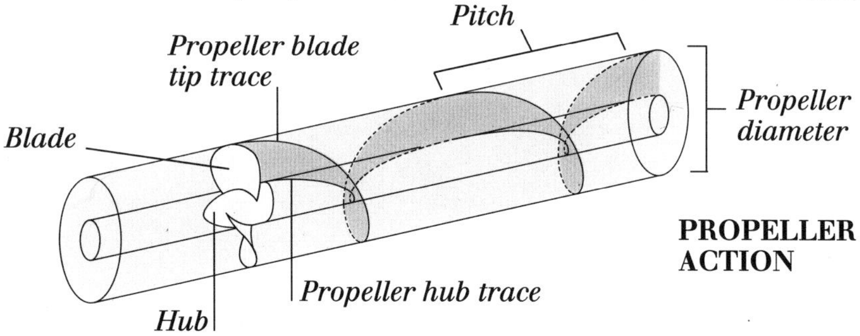

Strut

Frame

Piston rod (tail rod)

Stuffing box

Oscillating cylinder

Bottom plate (bedplate)

Slide valve rod

Control platform

Pitch

Propeller blade tip trace

Propeller diameter

Blade

Propeller hub trace

Hub

PROPELLER ACTION

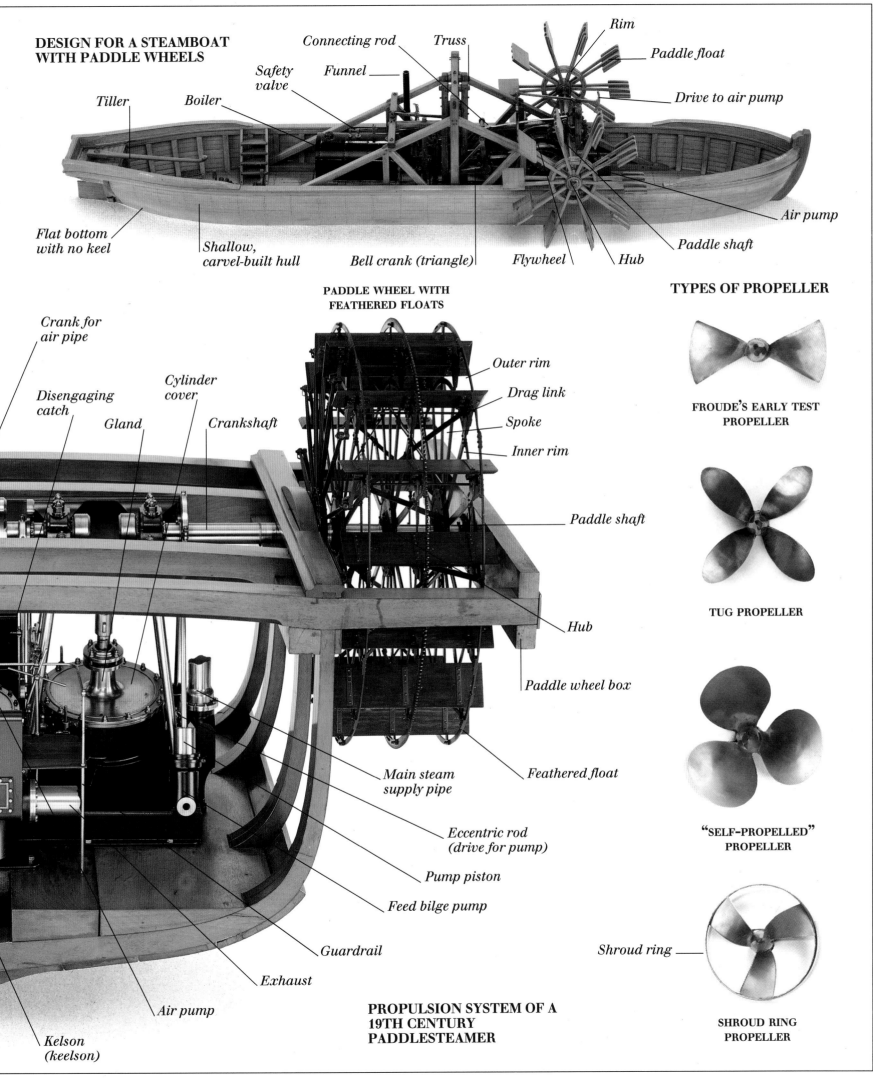

**DESIGN FOR A STEAMBOAT
WITH PADDLE WHEELS**

Connecting rod

Truss

Rim

Safety valve

Funnel

Paddle float

Tiller

Boiler

Drive to air pump

Flat bottom
with no keel

Shallow,
carvel-built hull

Bell crank (triangle)

Flywheel

Hub

Paddle shaft

Air pump

**PADDLE WHEEL WITH
FEATHERED FLOATS**

TYPES OF PROPELLER

Crank for
air pipe

Outer rim

Drag link

Disengaging
catch

Cylinder
cover

Spoke

Gland

Crankshaft

Inner rim

**FROUDE'S EARLY TEST
PROPELLER**

Paddle shaft

Hub

TUG PROPELLER

Paddle wheel box

Main steam
supply pipe

Feathered float

**"SELF-PROPELLED"
PROPELLER**

Eccentric rod
(drive for pump)

Pump piston

Feed bilge pump

Guardrail

Shroud ring

Exhaust

Air pump

**PROPULSION SYSTEM OF A
19TH CENTURY
PADDLESTEAMER**

**SHROUD RING
PROPELLER**

Kelson
(keelson)

The boat builder's yard

Traditionally, most small boats were built in a painstaking way by softening and shaping tropical hardwoods, and by fastening the planks (strakes) with copper rivets. Modern boats, in contrast, are often built of plywood or fiberglass, with epoxy resin glues, and synthetic rope and sail cloth. The 7 ft 6 in (2.3 m) marine plywood dinghy shown here, with its flat pram bow, is clinker-built—that is, built with overlapping strakes. It is made from a kit that includes a jig with molds over which the strakes are laid.

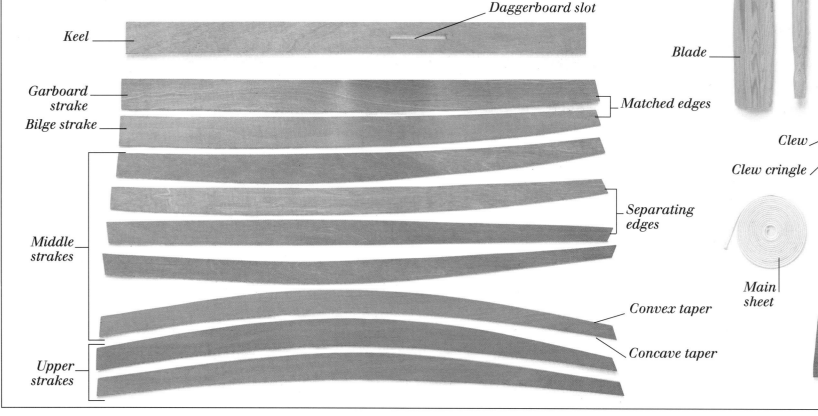

OARS

Peak cringle

Peak

Handle

BOAT BUILDING KIT WITH JIG

Gunwhale

Inwale

Transom knee (quarter knee)

Daggerboard case

Oar hole

Thwart knee

Seat support

Seat support

Apron knee

Mast step

Mast hole

Grooved reinforcement pad

Grooved reinforcement pad

Stern transom

Rudder

Station mold

Strongback (backbone)

Bow transom

Leech (leach)

Transom knee (quarter knee)

Tiller

Thwart knee

Station mold

Apron knee

Loom

PLANKING FOR ONE SIDE OF THE DINGHY

Daggerboard slot

Keel

Blade

Garboard strake

Bilge strake

Matched edges

Middle strakes

Separating edges

Convex taper

Concave taper

Clew

Clew cringle

Main sheet

Upper strakes

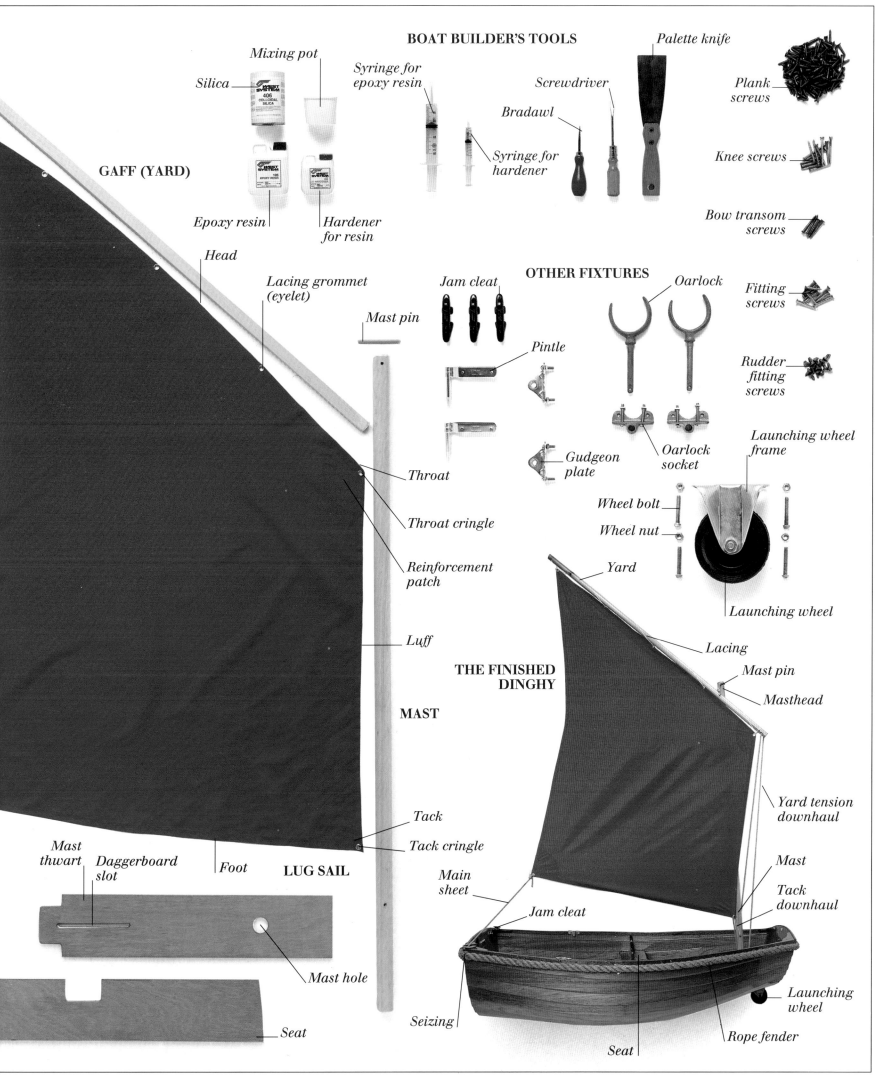

BOAT BUILDER'S TOOLS

Mixing pot

Silica

Syringe for epoxy resin

Screwdriver

Palette knife

Plank screws

Bradawl

Syringe for hardener

Knee screws

Epoxy resin

Hardener for resin

Bow transom screws

GAFF (YARD)

Head

Lacing grommet (eyelet)

OTHER FIXTURES

Jam cleat

Oarlock

Fitting screws

Mast pin

Pintle

Rudder fitting screws

Throat

Throat cringle

Gudgeon plate

Oarlock socket

Launching wheel frame

Wheel bolt

Wheel nut

Reinforcement patch

Yard

Launching wheel

Luff

THE FINISHED DINGHY

Lacing

Mast pin

Masthead

MAST

Yard tension downhaul

Tack

Tack cringle

Main sheet

Mast

Tack downhaul

Mast thwart

Daggerboard slot

Foot

LUG SAIL

Jam cleat

Mast hole

Launching wheel

Seizing

Rope fender

Seat

Seat

Rigging

MOST SAILING SHIPS HAVE TWO TYPES OF RIGGING. Standing rigging—kept taut by turnbuckles or old-fashioned lanyards and deadeyes—refers to the ropes, wires, and chains that support the masts and yards (horizontal spars). Running rigging, which includes types of block and tackle, halyards, and sheets, is used to hoist, lower, or trim sails.

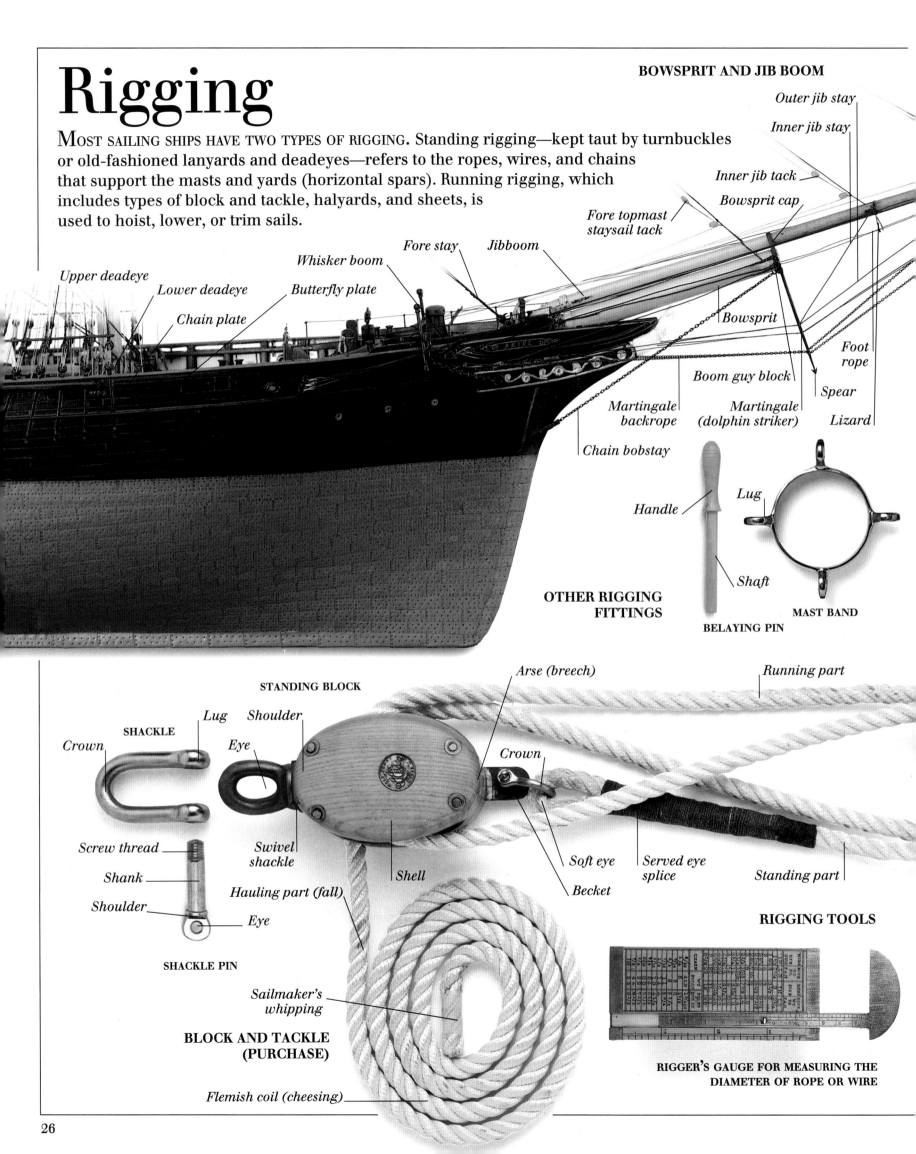

BOWSPRIT AND JIB BOOM

Outer jib stay

Inner jib stay

Inner jib tack

Bowsprit cap

Fore topmast staysail tack

Fore stay

Jibboom

Whisker boom

Butterfly plate

Upper deadeye

Lower deadeye

Chain plate

Bowsprit

Foot rope

Boom guy block

Spear

Martingale backrope

Martingale (dolphin striker)

Lizard

Chain bobstay

Handle

Lug

OTHER RIGGING FITTINGS

Shaft

BELAYING PIN

MAST BAND

STANDING BLOCK

Arse (breech)

Running part

Shoulder

Lug

SHACKLE

Crown

Eye

Crown

Screw thread

Swivel shackle

Soft eye

Served eye splice

Standing part

Shank

Shell

Becket

Shoulder

Hauling part (fall)

Eye

RIGGING TOOLS

SHACKLE PIN

Sailmaker's whipping

BLOCK AND TACKLE (PURCHASE)

RIGGER'S GAUGE FOR MEASURING THE DIAMETER OF ROPE OR WIRE

Flemish coil (cheesing)

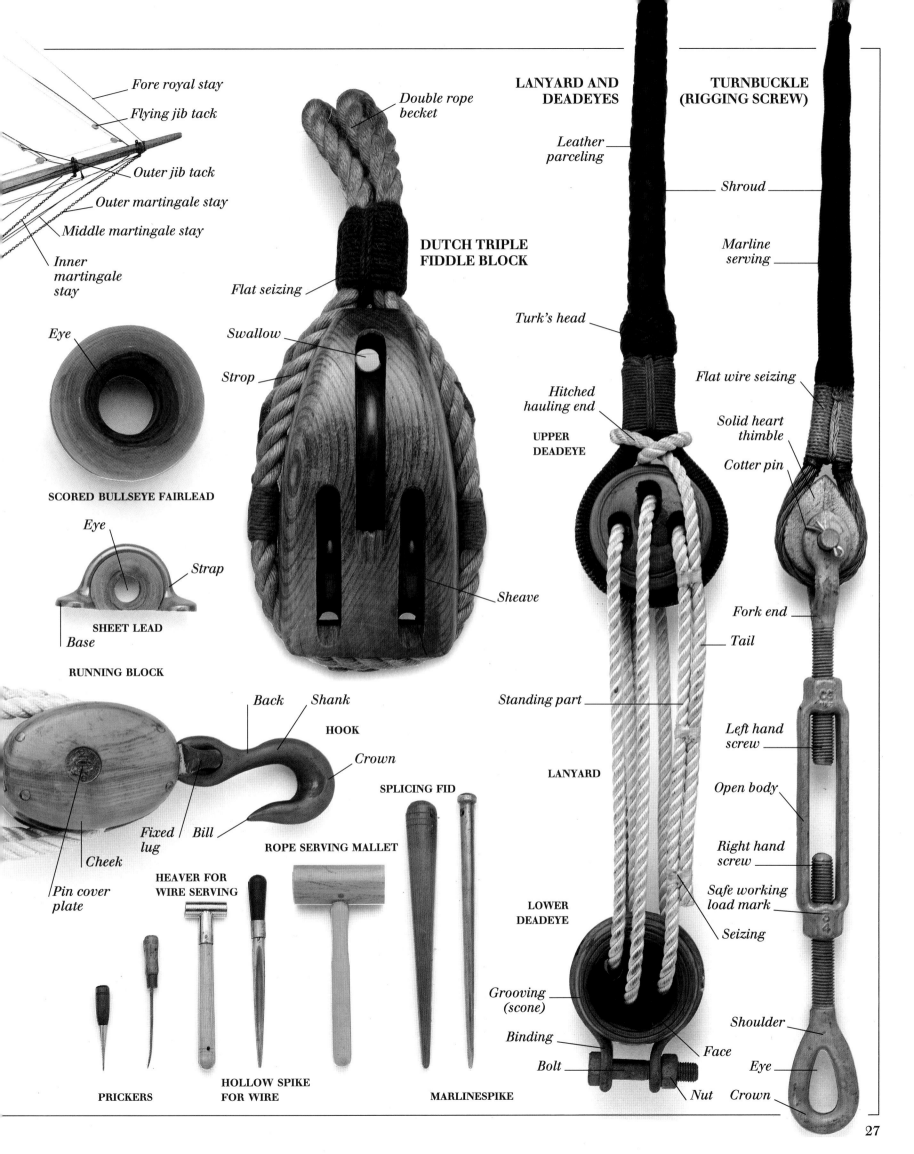

Fore royal stay

Flying jib tack

Outer jib tack

Outer martingale stay

Middle martingale stay

Inner martingale stay

Eye

SCORED BULLSEYE FAIRLEAD

Eye

Strap

SHEET LEAD

Base

RUNNING BLOCK

Double rope becket

DUTCH TRIPLE FIDDLE BLOCK

Flat seizing

Swallow

Strop

Sheave

Back   Shank

HOOK

Crown

Fixed lug   Bill

Cheek

Pin cover plate

SPLICING FID

ROPE SERVING MALLET

HEAVER FOR WIRE SERVING

PRICKERS

HOLLOW SPIKE FOR WIRE

MARLINESPIKE

LANYARD AND DEADEYES

TURNBUCKLE (RIGGING SCREW)

Leather parceling

Shroud

Marline serving

Turk's head

Hitched hauling end

UPPER DEADEYE

Flat wire seizing

Solid heart thimble

Cotter pin

Sheave

Fork end

Tail

Standing part

LANYARD

Left hand screw

Open body

Right hand screw

Safe working load mark

LOWER DEADEYE

Seizing

Grooving (scone)

Binding

Face

Bolt

Nut

Shoulder

Eye

Crown

Sails

THERE ARE TWO MAIN TYPES OF SAILS: Old-fashioned square sails hang from yards at right angles to the mast, and are powerful drivers with following winds; fore-and aft sails are set parallel to the length of the boat, with the luff (leading edge) of the sail attached to a mast or a stay. They are more efficient for all-round sailing, and almost all modern sailboats are rigged this way. Some fore-and-aft sails have a gaff at the head; Marconi-rig sails are pointed at the top (below). The bottom (foot) of the sail is on a boom. Sails are made of strips of cloth sewn together. Cotton and flax are traditional sail materials but synthetic fabrics are now more often used.

TOP OF A MARCONI SAIL

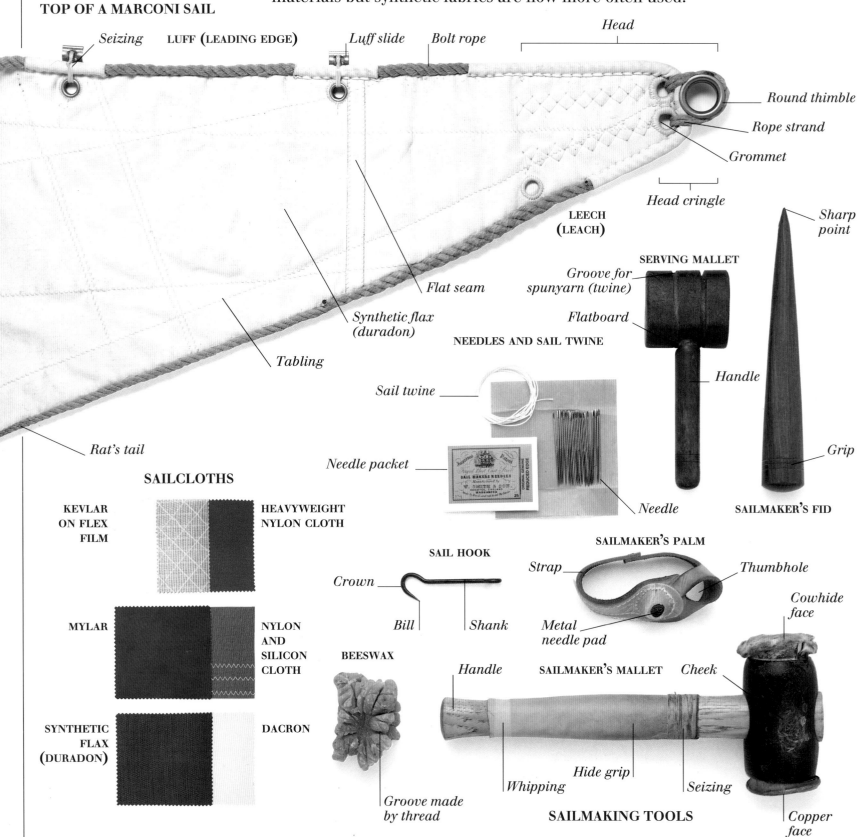

Seizing   LUFF (LEADING EDGE)   Luff slide   Bolt rope   Head

Round thimble

Rope strand

Grommet

Head cringle

LEECH (LEACH)

Flat seam

Synthetic flax (duradon)

Tabling

Rat's tail

Groove for spunyarn (twine)

SERVING MALLET

Flatboard

Handle

Sharp point

NEEDLES AND SAIL TWINE

Sail twine

Needle packet

Needle

Grip

SAILMAKER'S FID

SAILCLOTHS

KEVLAR ON FLEX FILM   HEAVYWEIGHT NYLON CLOTH

MYLAR   NYLON AND SILICON CLOTH

SAIL HOOK

Crown

Bill   Shank

SAILMAKER'S PALM

Strap   Thumbhole

Metal needle pad

Cowhide face

BEESWAX

Handle   SAILMAKER'S MALLET   Cheek

SYNTHETIC FLAX (DURADON)   DACRON

Whipping   Hide grip   Seizing

Groove made by thread

SAILMAKING TOOLS

Copper face

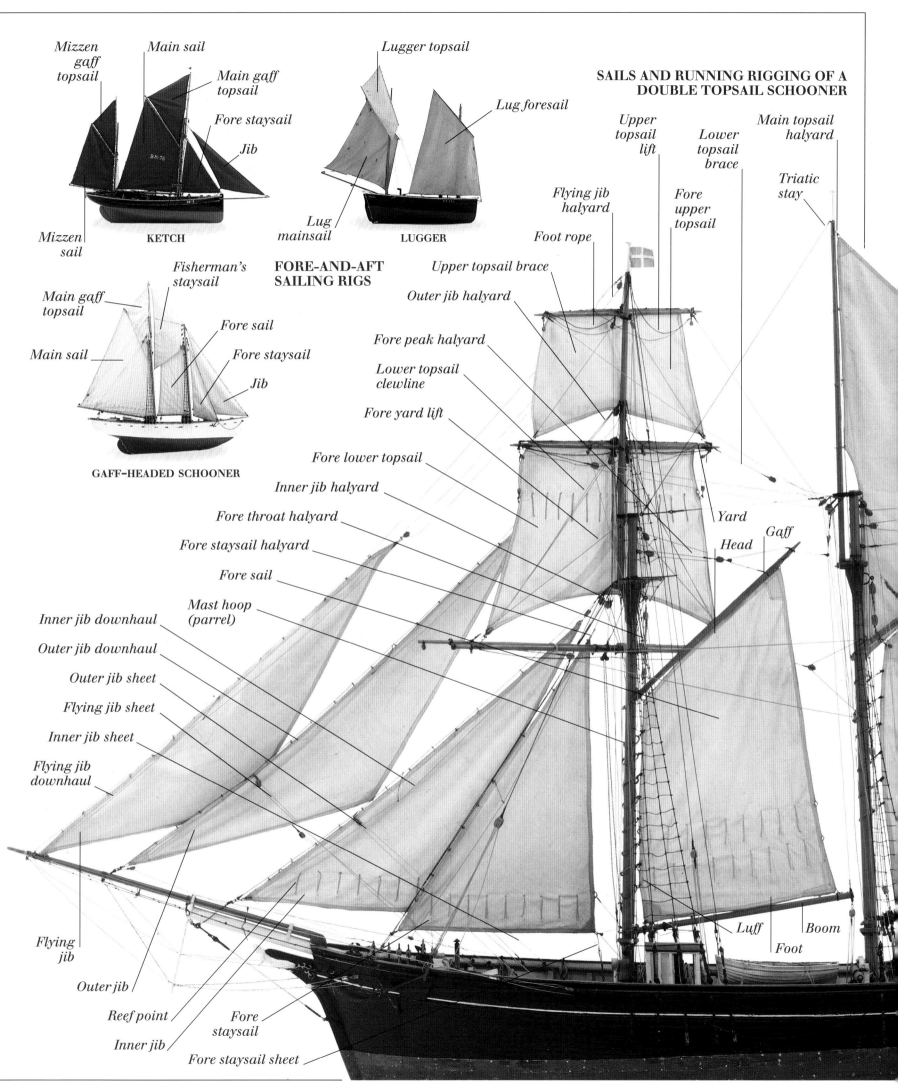

Mizzen gaff topsail

Main sail

Main gaff topsail

Fore staysail

Jib

BM-76

Mizzen sail

KETCH

Lugger topsail

Lug foresail

Lug mainsail

LUGGER

FORE-AND-AFT SAILING RIGS

Fisherman's staysail

Main gaff topsail

Fore sail

Main sail

Fore staysail

Jib

GAFF–HEADED SCHOONER

SAILS AND RUNNING RIGGING OF A DOUBLE TOPSAIL SCHOONER

Upper topsail lift

Lower topsail brace

Main topsail halyard

Flying jib halyard

Fore upper topsail

Triatic stay

Foot rope

Upper topsail brace

Outer jib halyard

Fore peak halyard

Lower topsail clewline

Fore yard lift

Fore lower topsail

Inner jib halyard

Fore throat halyard

Fore staysail halyard

Fore sail

Mast hoop (parrel)

Inner jib downhaul

Outer jib downhaul

Outer jib sheet

Flying jib sheet

Inner jib sheet

Flying jib downhaul

Flying jib

Outer jib

Reef point

Fore staysail

Inner jib

Fore staysail sheet

Yard

Head

Gaff

Luff

Boom

Foot

29

Man-powered craft

WHILE MANY MAN-POWERED CRAFT HAVE CHANGED LITTLE since the first boats, others have been developed for specific purposes, such as hauling goods, fishing, and sport. The cargo-carrying Bangladeshi dinghy is paddled or punted with a pole. The early Britons' coracle is still used for fishing. It is paddled over the bow with one hand only, while the other hand tends the fishing net. Most rowboats are rowed, or sculled, with a pair of oars worked in a continuous cycle of strokes. ("Sculling" can also mean to use just one oar over the stern of a small boat.) The scull shown at bottom is a super-light, fast sport craft with a sliding seat whose oars pivot on riggers to give more leverage. The canoe opposite has an outrigger to keep it from turning over.

Shoulder

Pintle

Captive socket

Crutch plate

TURNOVER OARLOCK   **UNEVEN OARLOCK**   **SQUARE PATTERN OARLOCK**

Quarter oar for steering

Stern

Goloi

Quarter oar pivot

Tie for quarter oar pivot

Woven split bamboo deck cover

BANGLADESHI DINGHY

POLE

PADDLE   *Blade*

SINGLE SCULLING BOAT AND OARS (WITH CLOTH DECKING REMOVED)

Neck

Spoon   *Blade*

Colors

Port-side oar

Adjusting screw

Gate clamp

Gate

Rigger

Sycamore beam

Grip

Starboard-side oar   *Button*   *Shaft*   *Loom*

Water shoot   *Shoe*   *Keel*

Bung   *Aft shoulder*   *Stretcher*

Sternpost   *Spruce beam*   *In-board*   *Diagonal frame*   *Aluminum beam*

Kelson (keelson)

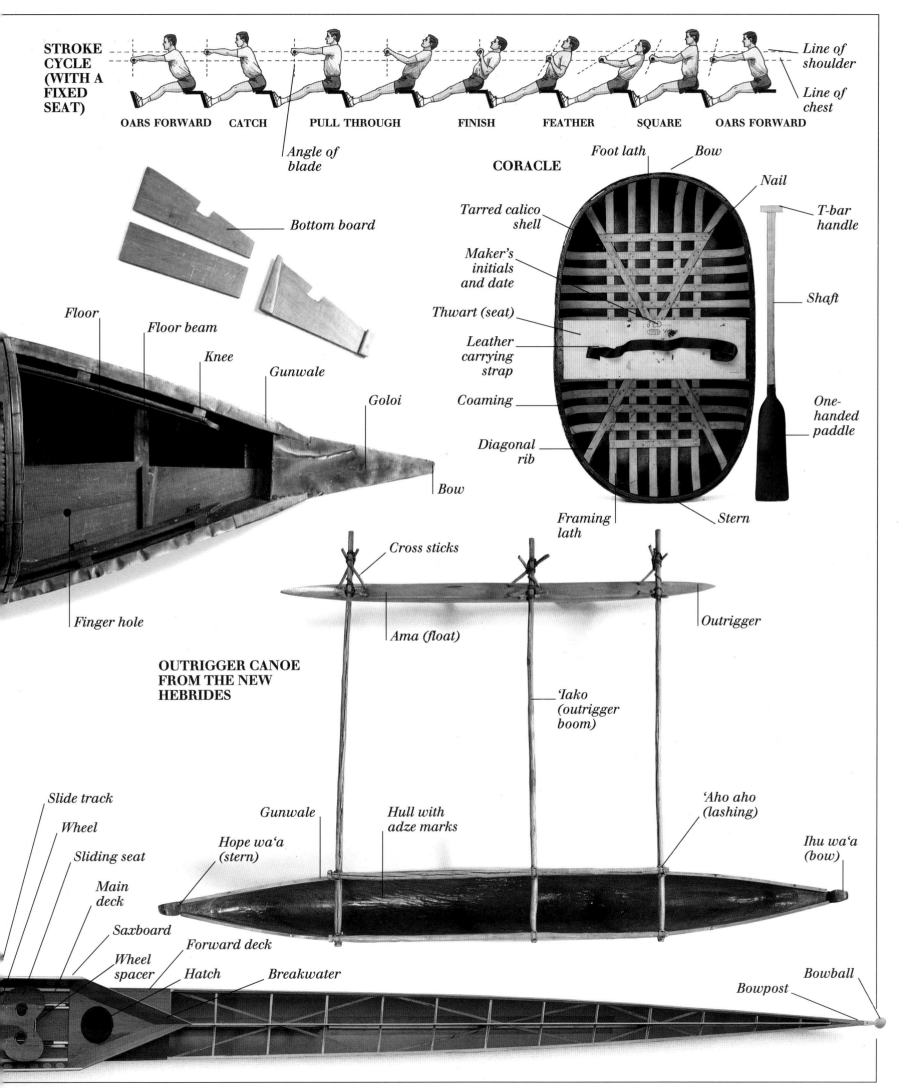

STROKE CYCLE (WITH A FIXED SEAT)

Line of shoulder

Line of chest

OARS FORWARD CATCH PULL THROUGH FINISH FEATHER SQUARE OARS FORWARD

Angle of blade

Bottom board

CORACLE

Foot lath

Bow

Nail

T-bar handle

Tarred calico shell

Maker's initials and date

Shaft

Thwart (seat)

Leather carrying strap

Coaming

One-handed paddle

Diagonal rib

Floor

Floor beam

Knee

Gunwale

Goloi

Framing lath

Stern

Bow

Finger hole

OUTRIGGER CANOE FROM THE NEW HEBRIDES

Cross sticks

Ama (float)

Outrigger

'Iako (outrigger boom)

Slide track

Wheel

Sliding seat

Main deck

Saxboard

Wheel spacer

Forward deck

Hatch

Breakwater

Gunwale

Hope wa'a (stern)

Hull with adze marks

'Aho aho (lashing)

Ihu wa'a (bow)

Bowball

Bowpost

31

Directions

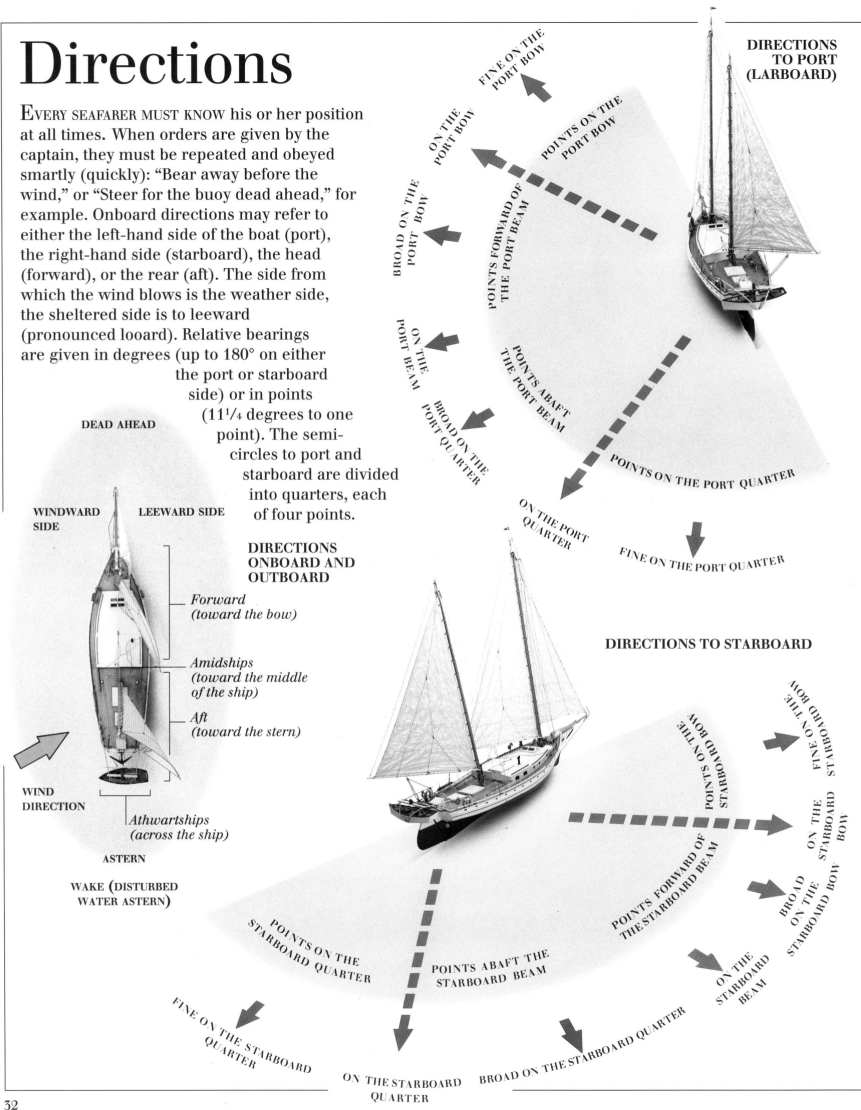

EVERY SEAFARER MUST KNOW his or her position at all times. When orders are given by the captain, they must be repeated and obeyed smartly (quickly): "Bear away before the wind," or "Steer for the buoy dead ahead," for example. Onboard directions may refer to either the left-hand side of the boat (port), the right-hand side (starboard), the head (forward), or the rear (aft). The side from which the wind blows is the weather side, the sheltered side is to leeward (pronounced looard). Relative bearings are given in degrees (up to 180° on either the port or starboard side) or in points (11¼ degrees to one point). The semi-circles to port and starboard are divided into quarters, each of four points.

DIRECTIONS TO PORT (LARBOARD)

FINE ON THE PORT BOW

ON THE PORT BOW

POINTS ON THE PORT BOW

BROAD ON THE PORT BOW

POINTS FORWARD OF THE PORT BEAM

ON THE PORT BEAM

POINTS ABAFT THE PORT BEAM

BROAD ON THE PORT QUARTER

POINTS ON THE PORT QUARTER

ON THE PORT QUARTER

FINE ON THE PORT QUARTER

DIRECTIONS ONBOARD AND OUTBOARD

DEAD AHEAD

WINDWARD SIDE

LEEWARD SIDE

Forward (toward the bow)

Amidships (toward the middle of the ship)

Aft (toward the stern)

Athwartships (across the ship)

WIND DIRECTION

ASTERN

WAKE (DISTURBED WATER ASTERN)

DIRECTIONS TO STARBOARD

FINE ON THE STARBOARD BOW

POINTS ON THE STARBOARD BOW

ON THE STARBOARD BOW

BROAD ON THE STARBOARD BOW

POINTS FORWARD OF THE STARBOARD BEAM

ON THE STARBOARD BEAM

POINTS ABAFT THE STARBOARD BEAM

BROAD ON THE STARBOARD QUARTER

POINTS ON THE STARBOARD QUARTER

ON THE STARBOARD QUARTER

FINE ON THE STARBOARD QUARTER

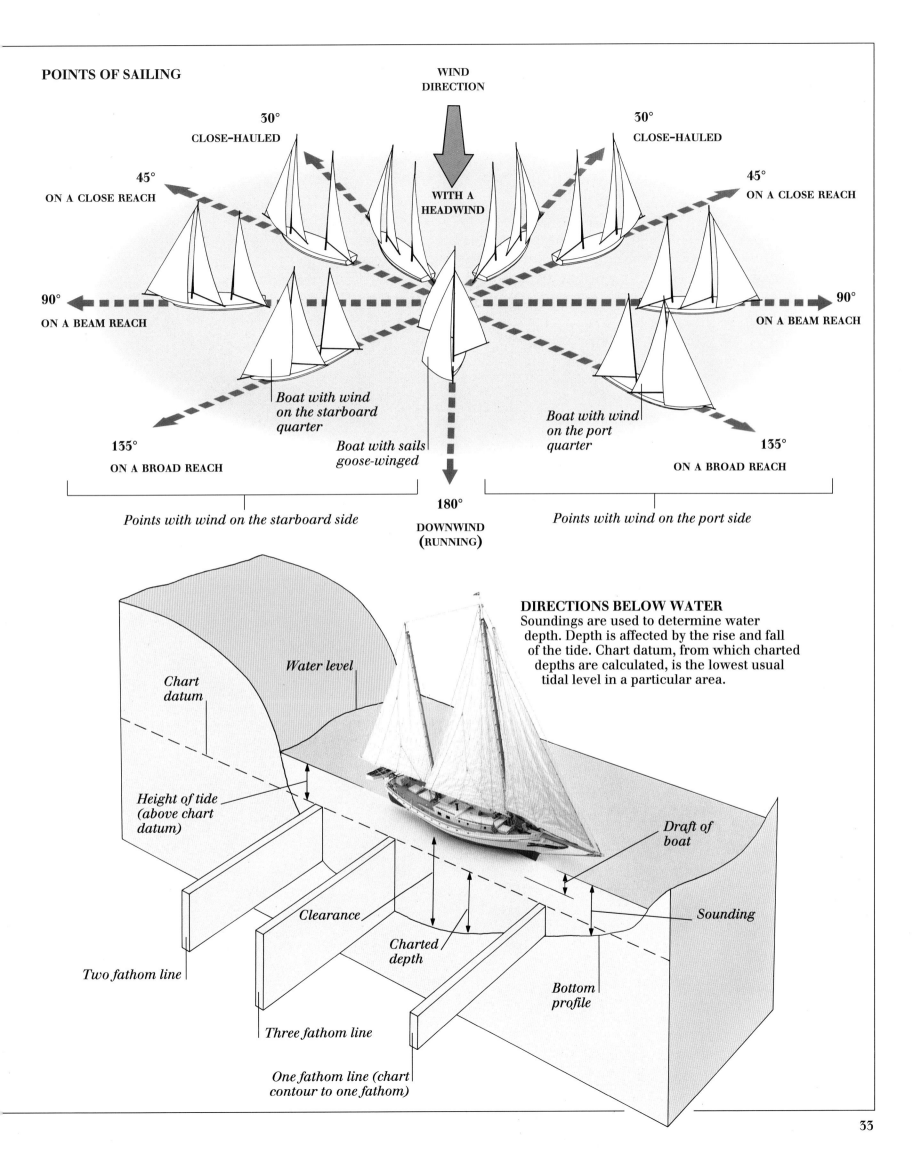

POINTS OF SAILING

WIND
DIRECTION

30°
CLOSE-HAULED

30°
CLOSE-HAULED

45°
ON A CLOSE REACH

45°
ON A CLOSE REACH

WITH A
HEADWIND

90°
ON A BEAM REACH

90°
ON A BEAM REACH

*Boat with wind
on the starboard
quarter*

*Boat with wind
on the port
quarter*

*Boat with sails
goose-winged*

135°
ON A BROAD REACH

135°
ON A BROAD REACH

180°
DOWNWIND
(RUNNING)

Points with wind on the starboard side

Points with wind on the port side

DIRECTIONS BELOW WATER
Soundings are used to determine water
depth. Depth is affected by the rise and fall
of the tide. Chart datum, from which charted
depths are calculated, is the lowest usual
tidal level in a particular area.

Water level

*Chart
datum*

*Height of tide
(above chart
datum)*

*Draft of
boat*

Sounding

Clearance

*Charted
depth*

Two fathom line

*Bottom
profile*

Three fathom line

*One fathom line (chart
contour to one fathom)*

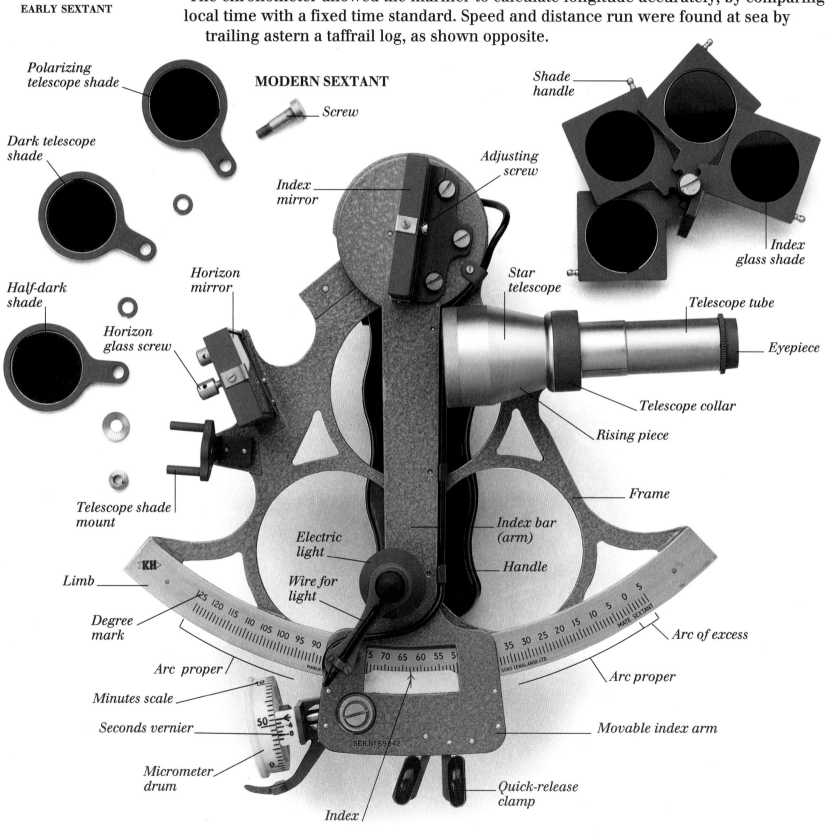

Navigation

NAVIGATION IS THE ART OF GUIDING A SHIP SAFELY between two points defined in terms of their latitude and longitude. Sailors in early times relied on landmarks for direction, while the watchkeeper turned an hourglass to indicate how long the ship had been following a given compass course. Like the cross-stave and the astrolabe, the sextant enabled sailors to measure their latitude by showing the angle between two known objects or between a heavenly body and the horizon. The chronometer allowed the mariner to calculate longitude accurately, by comparing local time with a fixed time standard. Speed and distance run were found at sea by trailing astern a taffrail log, as shown opposite.

Telescope

Limb

EARLY SEXTANT

Polarizing telescope shade

Dark telescope shade

Half-dark shade

MODERN SEXTANT

Screw

Index mirror

Adjusting screw

Shade handle

Index glass shade

Star telescope

Telescope tube

Eyepiece

Telescope collar

Rising piece

Horizon mirror

Horizon glass screw

Telescope shade mount

Frame

Index bar (arm)

Handle

Electric light

Wire for light

Limb

Degree mark

Arc proper

Minutes scale

Seconds vernier

Micrometer drum

Index

Arc of excess

Arc proper

Movable index arm

Quick-release clamp

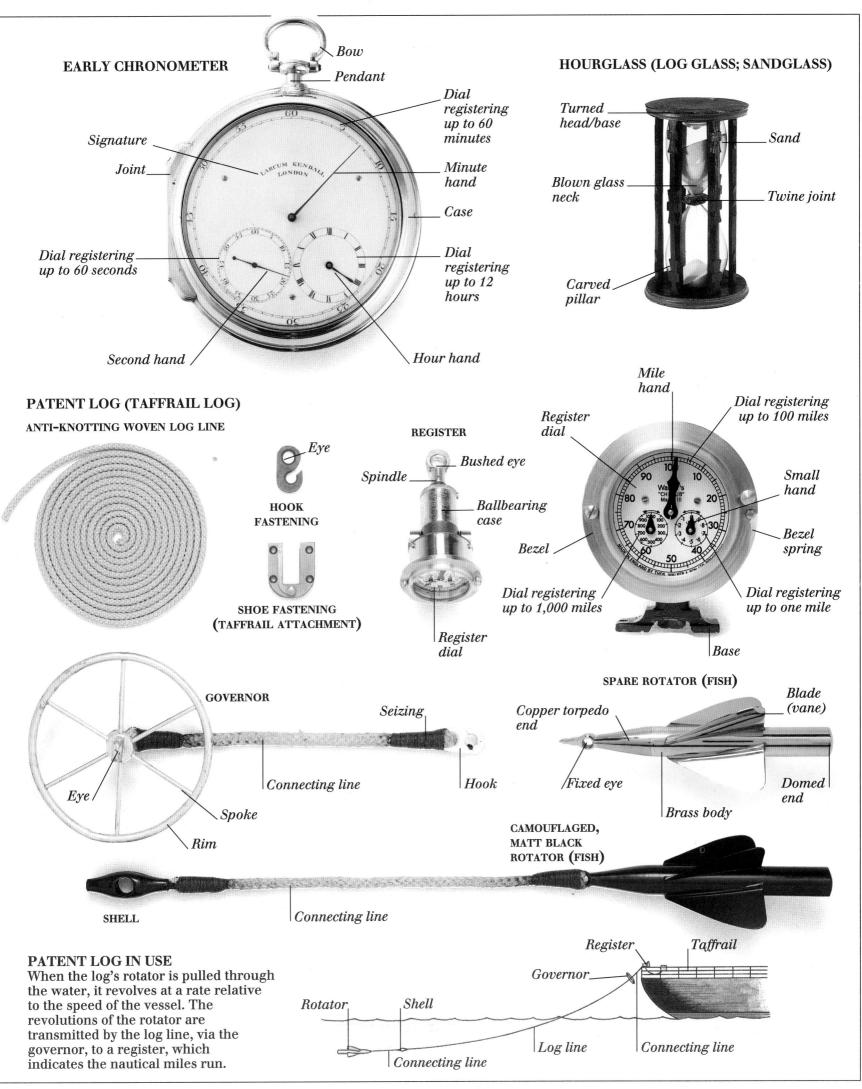

EARLY CHRONOMETER

Bow

Pendant

Dial registering up to 60 minutes

Signature

Joint

Minute hand

Case

Dial registering up to 60 seconds

Dial registering up to 12 hours

Second hand

Hour hand

HOURGLASS (LOG GLASS; SANDGLASS)

Turned head/base

Sand

Blown glass neck

Twine joint

Carved pillar

PATENT LOG (TAFFRAIL LOG)

ANTI-KNOTTING WOVEN LOG LINE

Eye

HOOK FASTENING

SHOE FASTENING (TAFFRAIL ATTACHMENT)

REGISTER

Bushed eye

Spindle

Ballbearing case

Register dial

Register dial

Mile hand

Dial registering up to 100 miles

Register dial

Small hand

Bezel

Bezel spring

Dial registering up to 1,000 miles

Dial registering up to one mile

Base

GOVERNOR

Seizing

Connecting line

Hook

Eye

Spoke

Rim

SPARE ROTATOR (FISH)

Blade (vane)

Copper torpedo end

Fixed eye

Brass body

Domed end

CAMOUFLAGED, MATT BLACK ROTATOR (FISH)

Connecting line

SHELL

PATENT LOG IN USE

When the log's rotator is pulled through the water, it revolves at a rate relative to the speed of the vessel. The revolutions of the rotator are transmitted by the log line, via the governor, to a register, which indicates the nautical miles run.

Register

Taffrail

Governor

Rotator

Shell

Log line

Connecting line

Connecting line

Piloting

NAVIGATING A SHIP in waters where charted landmarks, lighthouses, or buoys are visible is the art of piloting. Mariners have many aids to help them find their way when piloting. The magnetic compass is based on the attraction of a magnet to magnetic north. A round compass card rests on a pivot, held steady by magnetism; it is marked with 360° or a series of directional "points." These indicate the ship's course. The compass is often housed in a binnacle, a wooden case with correctors that counter the magnetic distortion of an iron ship. Most vessels now use electronic devices to find water depth, but some still use the lead line, marked in fathoms. (A fathom is six feet.) Terms such as "and a half one" indicate fractions of a fathom. Lighthouses flash lights in regular sequences that are marked on nautical charts. Buoys are floating marks that warn of dangers or show safe channels. Shape, color, and sometimes "top-marks" distinguish one buoy from another. Those shown opposite are commonly found in European waters.

Pivot
Mounting bracket
Compass card
Safety chain
Lubber's line

MAGNETIC COMPASS

18TH CENTURY COMPASS

North cardinal point
North north east mark
North east cardinal point
Date of manufacture
North west cardinal point
Compass card
West cardinal point
East cardinal point
Compass bowl
Cap and pivot
South east cardinal point
South west cardinal point
Maker's address
Degrees notation
South cardinal point
Lubber's line

BINNACLE

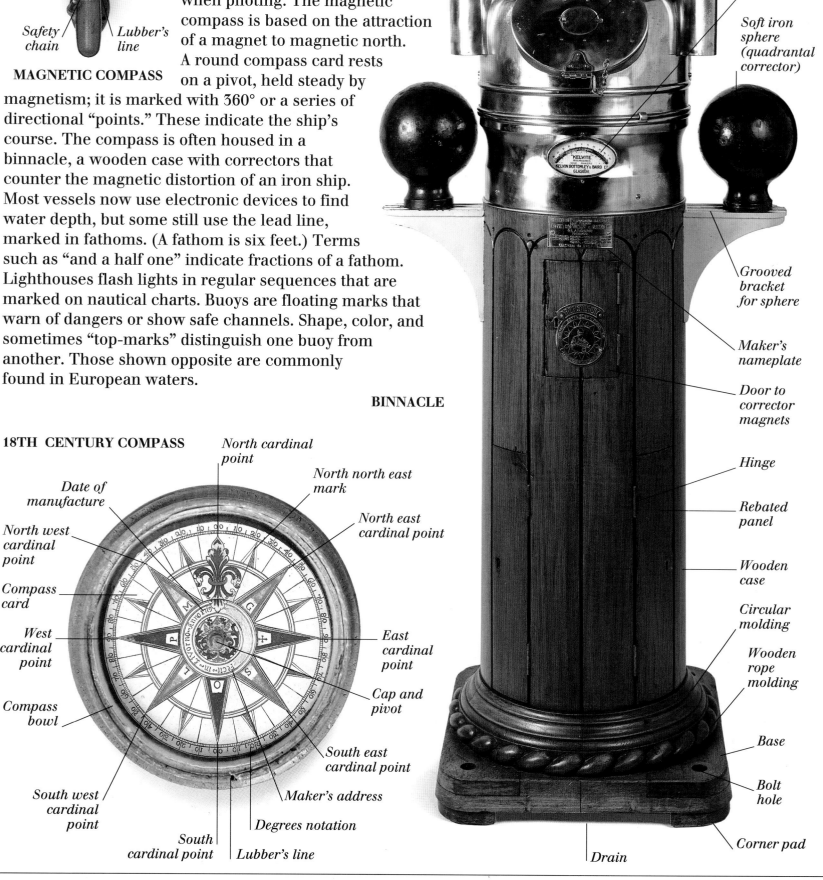

Hood (cowl)
Shutter covering compass card
Lamp receptacle
Clinometer
Soft iron sphere (quadrantal corrector)
Grooved bracket for sphere
Maker's nameplate
Door to corrector magnets
Hinge
Rebated panel
Wooden case
Circular molding
Wooden rope molding
Base
Bolt hole
Corner pad
Drain

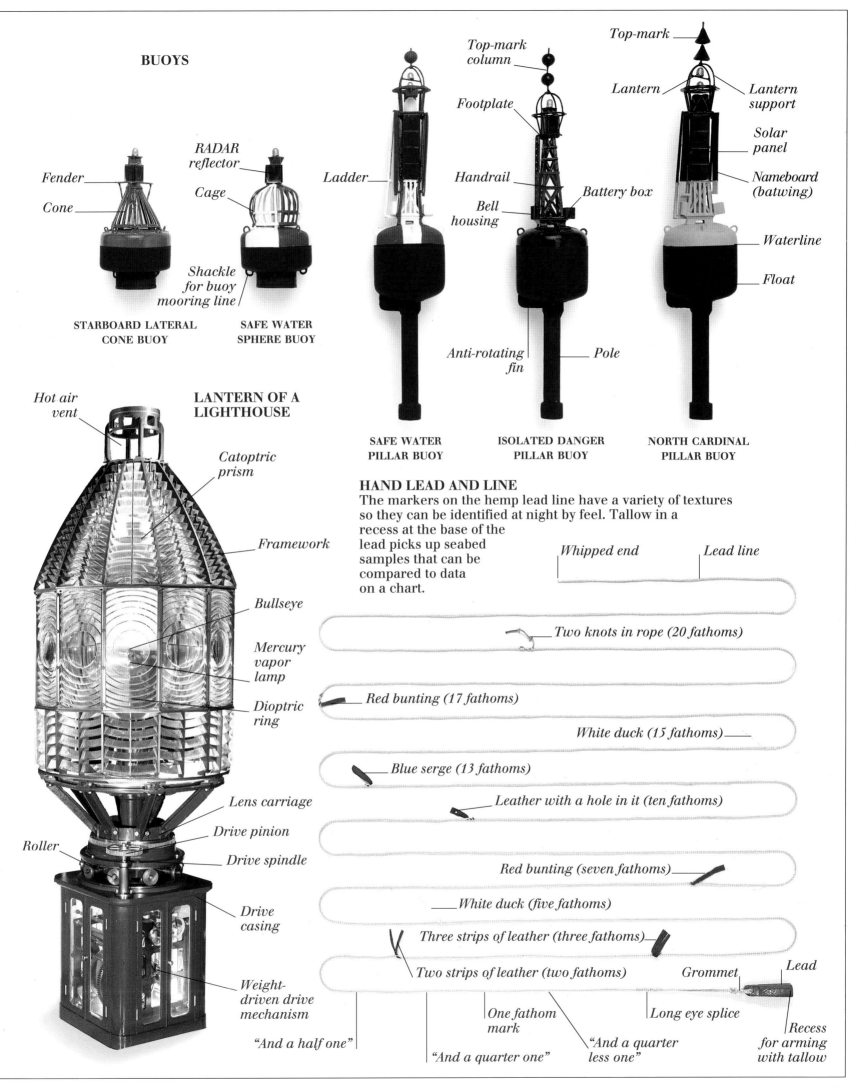

BUOYS

Fender

Cone

RADAR reflector

Cage

Shackle for buoy mooring line

STARBOARD LATERAL CONE BUOY

SAFE WATER SPHERE BUOY

Top-mark column

Footplate

Ladder

Handrail

Bell housing

Battery box

Top-mark

Lantern

Lantern support

Solar panel

Nameboard (batwing)

Waterline

Float

Anti-rotating fin

Pole

SAFE WATER PILLAR BUOY

ISOLATED DANGER PILLAR BUOY

NORTH CARDINAL PILLAR BUOY

LANTERN OF A LIGHTHOUSE

Hot air vent

Catoptric prism

Framework

Bullseye

Mercury vapor lamp

Dioptric ring

Lens carriage

Drive pinion

Roller

Drive spindle

Drive casing

Weight-driven drive mechanism

HAND LEAD AND LINE
The markers on the hemp lead line have a variety of textures so they can be identified at night by feel. Tallow in a recess at the base of the lead picks up seabed samples that can be compared to data on a chart.

Whipped end

Lead line

Two knots in rope (20 fathoms)

Red bunting (17 fathoms)

White duck (15 fathoms)

Blue serge (13 fathoms)

Leather with a hole in it (ten fathoms)

Red bunting (seven fathoms)

White duck (five fathoms)

Three strips of leather (three fathoms)

Two strips of leather (two fathoms)

Grommet

Lead

One fathom mark

Long eye splice

"And a half one"

"And a quarter one"

"And a quarter less one"

Recess for arming with tallow

Charts and piloting tools

EARLY SEAFARERS COULD CALCULATE THEIR LATITUDE by observing the altitude of certain stars identified from a celestial globe. Modern charts show lines of latitude (parallels)—measured in degrees, minutes, and seconds north or south of the equator—and lines of longitude (meridians)—measured east or west from zero longitude at Greenwich, England. A rhumb line intersects all meridians at the same angle; to follow a rhumb line ensures that the navigator keeps a constant course. The chart also shows sea depths, coastlines, shore elevations, lights, buoys, and other features identifiable from a ship. Parallel rulers and the plotter are used in working out courses on a chart, while dividers help measure the distance between charted points. The hand-bearing compass has a sight that a navigator lines up with visible objects, so as to obtain their compass bearings. True north is at the North Pole; note that magnetic north (to which a compass needle points) is actually in the middle of the Canadian Arctic.

DIVIDERS

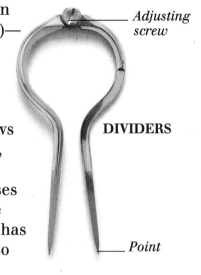

Adjusting screw

Point

CELESTIAL GLOBE

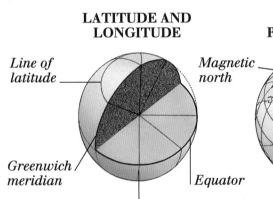

Constellation symbol

Meridian line

Equator

Stand

LATITUDE AND LONGITUDE

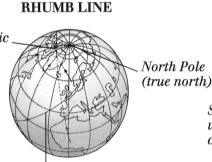

Line of latitude

Greenwich meridian

Line of longitude

Equator

RHUMB LINE

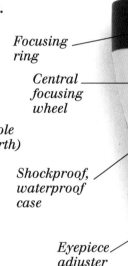

Magnetic north

North Pole (true north)

Rhumb line

BINOCULARS

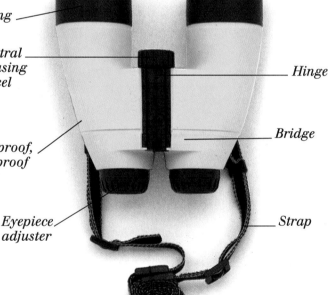

Eyepiece

Focusing ring

Central focusing wheel

Hinge

Bridge

Shockproof, waterproof case

Eyepiece adjuster

Strap

HAND-BEARING COMPASS

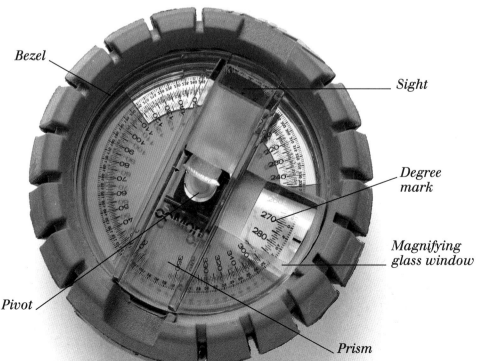

Bezel

Sight

Degree mark

Magnifying glass window

Pivot

Prism

BRETON PLOTTER AND NOTEPAD

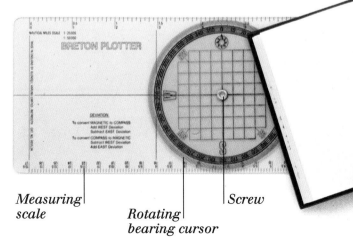

BRETON PLOTTER

DEVIATION
To convert MAGNETIC to COMPASS
Add WEST Deviation
Subtract EAST Deviation
To convert COMPASS to MAGNETIC
Subtract WEST Deviation
Add EAST Deviation

Measuring scale

Rotating bearing cursor

Screw

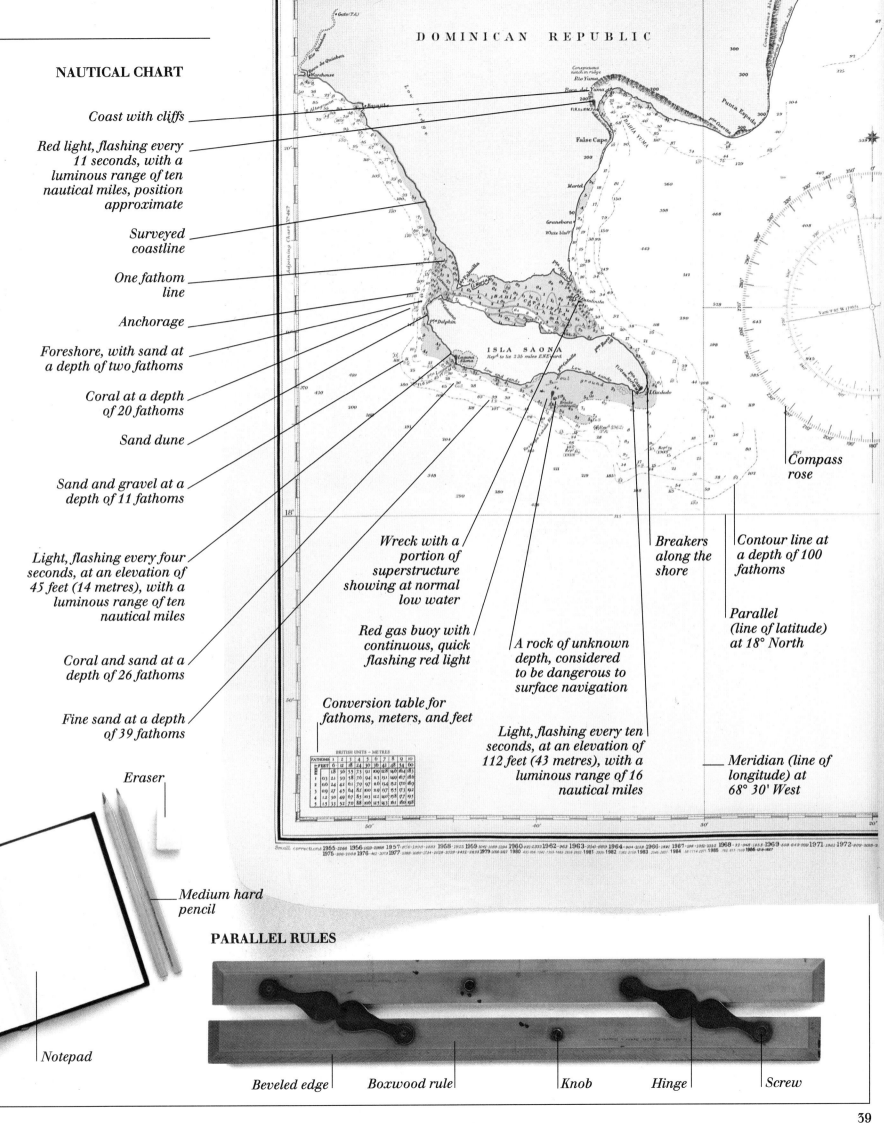

NAUTICAL CHART

Coast with cliffs

Red light, flashing every 11 seconds, with a luminous range of ten nautical miles, position approximate

Surveyed coastline

One fathom line

Anchorage

Foreshore, with sand at a depth of two fathoms

Coral at a depth of 20 fathoms

Sand dune

Sand and gravel at a depth of 11 fathoms

Light, flashing every four seconds, at an elevation of 45 feet (14 metres), with a luminous range of ten nautical miles

Coral and sand at a depth of 26 fathoms

Fine sand at a depth of 39 fathoms

Wreck with a portion of superstructure showing at normal low water

Red gas buoy with continuous, quick flashing red light

Conversion table for fathoms, meters, and feet

A rock of unknown depth, considered to be dangerous to surface navigation

Light, flashing every ten seconds, at an elevation of 112 feet (43 metres), with a luminous range of 16 nautical miles

Breakers along the shore

Contour line at a depth of 100 fathoms

Parallel (line of latitude) at 18° North

Meridian (line of longitude) at 68° 30' West

Compass rose

Eraser

Medium hard pencil

Notepad

DOMINICAN REPUBLIC

ISLA SAONA

PARALLEL RULES

Beveled edge

Boxwood rule

Knob

Hinge

Screw

Flags

FOR CENTURIES, FLAGS HAVE BEEN USED TO IDENTIFY SHIPS and to pass messages from one vessel to another—either friend or foe. Each signal flag or combination of flags has a different meaning, which on sailing vessels can be changed by hoisting them on different masts. Flags are still important on ships today; national flags or ensigns identify a ship's country of origin, and standardized alphabet and number flags can be used to spell out messages. The flag of a country whose waters a ship is entering must be flown as a matter of courtesy. Solo international code flags convey specific messages, as shown on the opposite page. Other flag systems are meant for specialized jobs. For example, signalers still sometimes use semaphore code to pass messages over short distances.

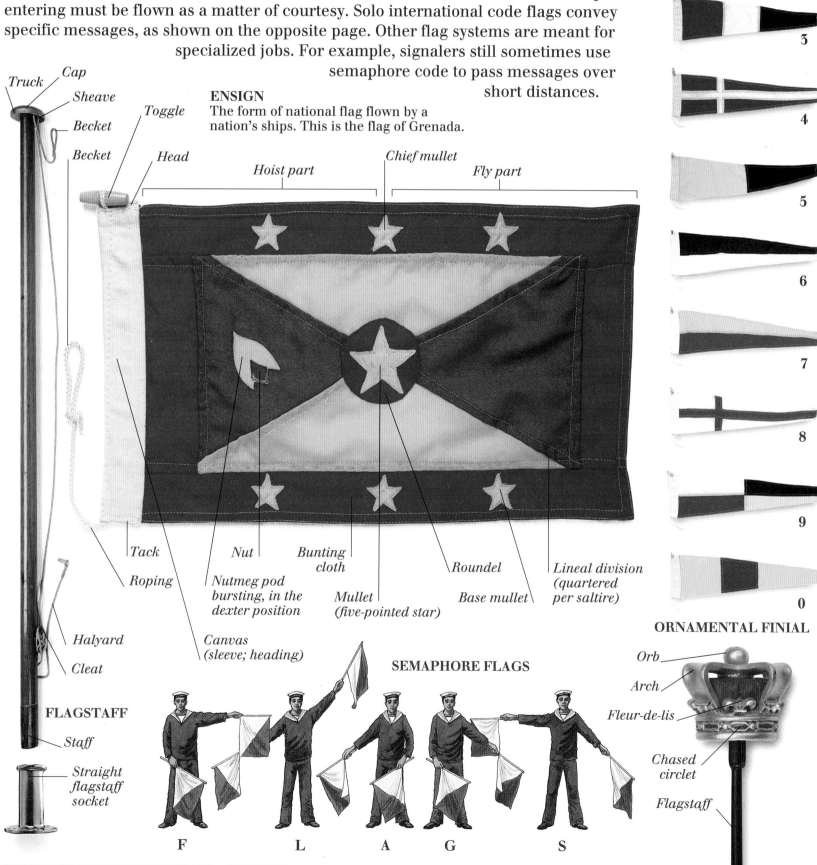

ENSIGN
The form of national flag flown by a nation's ships. This is the flag of Grenada.

Truck
Cap
Sheave
Becket
Becket
Toggle
Head
Hoist part
Chief mullet
Fly part
Tack
Nut
Bunting cloth
Roundel
Lineal division (quartered per saltire)
Roping
Nutmeg pod bursting, in the dexter position
Mullet (five-pointed star)
Base mullet
Canvas (sleeve; heading)
Halyard
Cleat

FLAGSTAFF
Staff
Straight flagstaff socket

SEMAPHORE FLAGS

F   L   A   G   S

1
2
3
4
5
6
7
8
9
0

ORNAMENTAL FINIAL
Orb
Arch
Fleur-de-lis
Chased circlet
Flagstaff

A

KEEP WELL CLEAR
AT LOW SPEED

B

I AM CARRYING
DANGEROUS GOODS

C

YES (AFFIRMATIVE)

D

I AM MANEUVERING
WITH DIFFICULTY

E

I AM DIRECTING MY
COURSE TO STARBOARD

F

I AM DISABLED;
COMMUNICATE WITH ME

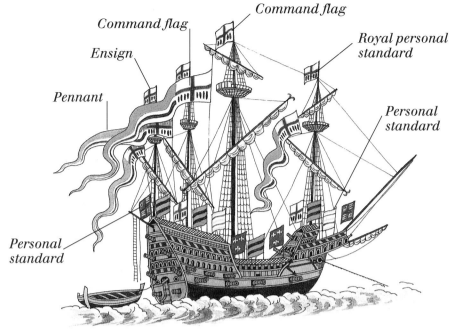

A DRESSED SHIP SHOWING FLAG POSITIONS

G

I REQUIRE A PILOT

H

I HAVE A PILOT
ON BOARD

I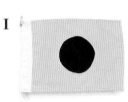

I AM DIRECTING MY
COURSE TO PORT

J

I AM ON FIRE; KEEP
CLEAR OF ME

K

I HAVE SOMETHING
TO COMMUNICATE

L

YOU SHOULD STOP
YOUR VESSEL

M

MY VESSEL IS STOPPED

N

NO (NEGATIVE)

O

MAN OVERBOARD

P

ALL PERSONS TO
REPORT ON BOARD

Q

I REQUEST FREE
PRATIQUE

R

NO MEANING

S

MY ENGINES ARE GOING
FULL SPEED ASTERN

T

KEEP CLEAR OF ME

U

YOU ARE RUNNING
INTO DANGER

V

I REQUIRE ASSISTANCE

W

I REQUIRE MEDICAL
ASSISTANCE

X

STOP CARRYING OUT
YOUR INTENTIONS

Y

I AM DRAGGING
MY ANCHOR

Z

I REQUIRE A TUG

ANSWERING PENNANT

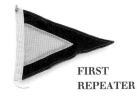

FIRST
REPEATER

SECOND
REPEATER

THIRD
REPEATER

41

Signals

LIKE FLAGS, SOUND AND LIGHT SIGNALS are used to inform other vessels of a ship's movements. Signaling systems overlap and are complementary to one another. The Very pistol was designed to fire pyrotechnic lights of various colors and patterns that conveyed messages to other craft or to the shore. Today, the Very pistol is sometimes used to fire distress signals. Morse code is a language of dots and dashes that spells out messages when produced by sound or light. The interval of one dash is equal to three dots. The Aldis lamp sends light messages in morse code by means of a trigger-operated shutter. Calls made on a boatswain's pipe pass orders and information to a ship's crew. Navigation lights, or running lights, identify the port and starboard sides of a ship at night. In poor visibility, the fog horn must be sounded; combinations of short and long blasts convey particular meanings. When helping another ship to moor or come alongside, sailors use a code of hand signals, shown opposite. The ship's bell is used primarily to signal the time.

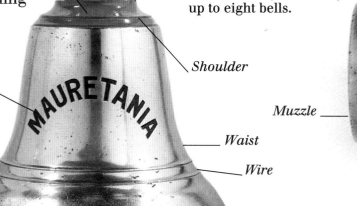

Crown
Wire
Engraved lettering
MAURETANIA

SHIP'S BELL
Throughout each four-hour watch, hours and half-hours are struck by a ship's bell. The time is described as "one bell" for the first half hour, "two bells" for the second half hour, and so on, up to eight bells.

Shoulder
Waist
Wire
Lip
Mouth

Muzzle
Barrel

MORSE CODE

A • ▬
B ▬ • • •
C ▬ • ▬ •
D ▬ • •
E •
F • • ▬ •
G ▬ ▬ •
H • • • •
I • •

J • ▬ ▬ ▬
K ▬ • ▬
L • ▬ • •
M ▬ ▬
N ▬ •
O ▬ ▬ ▬
P • ▬ ▬ •
Q ▬ ▬ • ▬
R • ▬ •

R • ▬ •
S • • •
T ▬
U • • ▬
V • • • ▬
W • ▬ ▬
X ▬ • • ▬
Y ▬ • ▬ ▬
Z ▬ ▬ • •

ALDIS LAMP
This lamp has been partially dismantled to show the reflector housing.

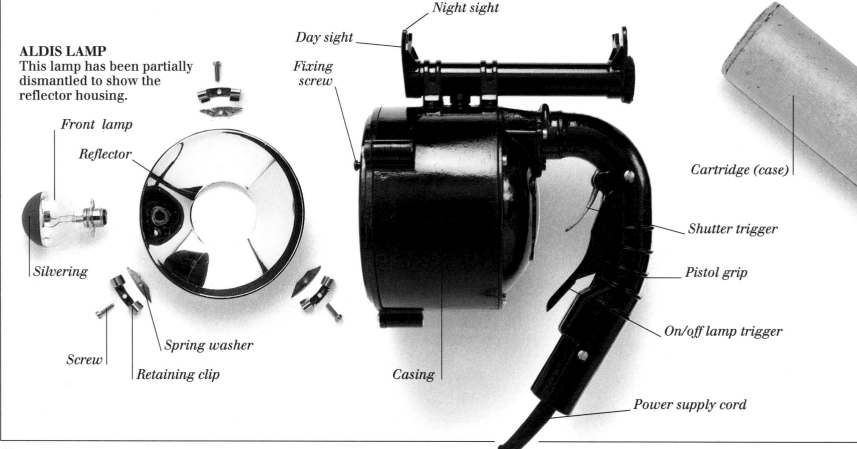

Night sight
Day sight
Fixing screw

Front lamp
Reflector
Silvering
Screw
Spring washer
Retaining clip
Casing

Cartridge (case)
Shutter trigger
Pistol grip
On/off lamp trigger
Power supply cord

VERY PISTOL (SIGNALING PISTOL)

Flashguard (lug)

Chamber

Extractor

Extractor pin

Stirrup

Hammer

Stirrup fastening screw

WEBLEY & SCOTT LTD
LONDON & BIRMINGHAM
'15

Joint axis pin

Body (frame)

Hammer screw

Pistol mark

Maker's name

Trigger

Year of acceptance into ship's stores

Government inspector's mark

Trigger guard

Trigger screw

Stock screw

Stock (grip)

Rim

Butt

Metal sleeve (head)

Butt swivel (butt lanyard ring)

FOG HORN

Button

Pipe

Bell

Dioptric lens

Port side lens

Gas bottle

Starboard side lens

Spiral tungsten halogen bulb

Base

NAVIGATION (RUNNING) LIGHT

Gun

Buoy

Inscription

Hole

Mouthpiece

Shackle

Keel

BOATSWAIN'S PIPE (CALL)
This whistle has two main notes
—a "low" and a "high"—and
three tones—a "plain", a "warble",
and a "trill".

GANGWAY HAND SIGNALS

CARRY ON

LIE OFF

Boatswain's pipe

MAKE FAST

COME ALONGSIDE

Gangway

The life raft

IT IS CRUCIAL THAT ALL VESSELS be equipped with the lifesaving gear appropriate to their sailing conditions. The life raft shown here is designed to hold four people in the roughest seas. It inflates quickly, avoids capsizing, and maintains the body heat of those aboard. It should be tied to the ship by a rope called a painter. In an emergency, the crew throws the deflated raft overboard and tugs on the painter, which releases carbon dioxide from a cylinder and inflates the raft. Once aboard, the crew cuts the painter, releases the drogue (sea anchor), opens the emergency pack, and starts looking for land or another ship.

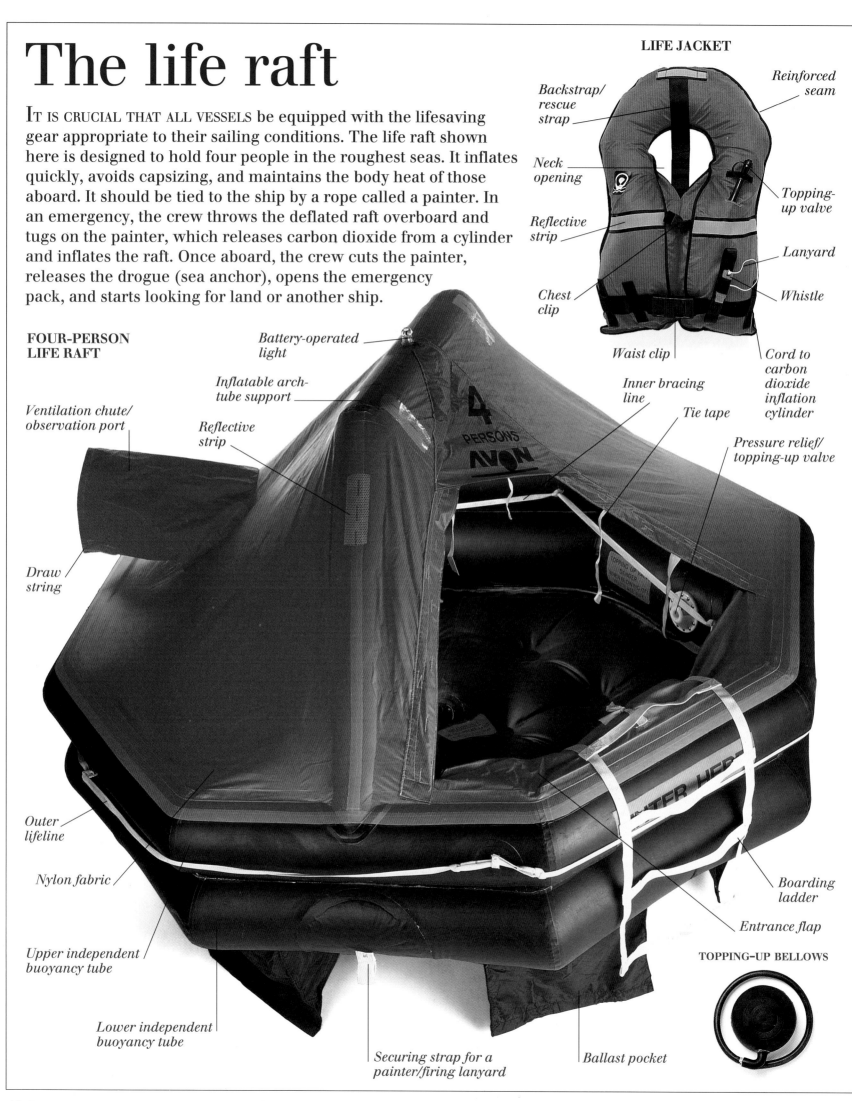

LIFE JACKET

Backstrap/ rescue strap

Reinforced seam

Neck opening

Topping- up valve

Reflective strip

Lanyard

Chest clip

Whistle

Waist clip

Cord to carbon dioxide inflation cylinder

FOUR-PERSON LIFE RAFT

Battery-operated light

Inflatable arch- tube support

Inner bracing line

Tie tape

Ventilation chute/ observation port

Reflective strip

Pressure relief/ topping-up valve

Draw string

Outer lifeline

Nylon fabric

Boarding ladder

Entrance flap

Upper independent buoyancy tube

TOPPING-UP BELLOWS

Lower independent buoyancy tube

Securing strap for a painter/firing lanyard

Ballast pocket

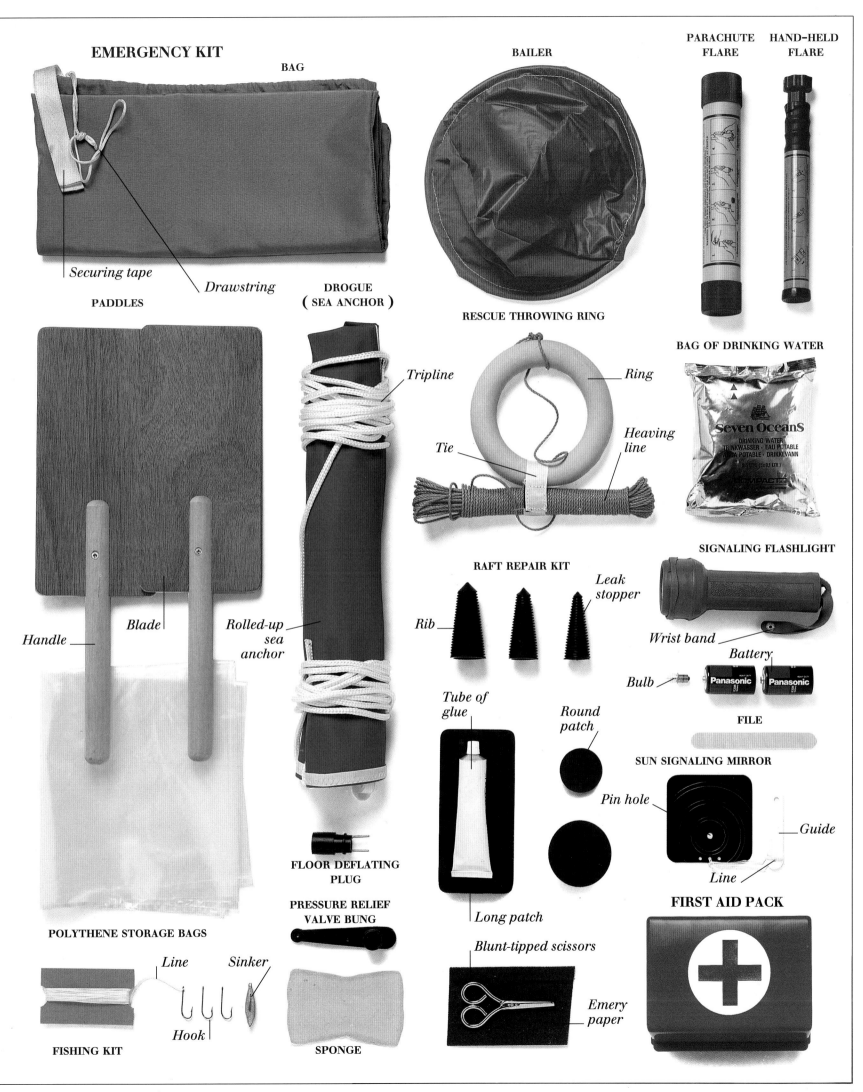

EMERGENCY KIT

BAG

Securing tape

Drawstring

BAILER

PARACHUTE FLARE

HAND-HELD FLARE

PADDLES

DROGUE (SEA ANCHOR)

RESCUE THROWING RING

Tripline

Ring

Tie

Heaving line

BAG OF DRINKING WATER

Seven Oceans
DRINKING WATER
TRINKWASSER · EAU POTABLE
AGUA POTABLE · DRIKKEVANN

Handle

Blade

Rolled-up sea anchor

RAFT REPAIR KIT

Leak stopper

Rib

SIGNALING FLASHLIGHT

Wrist band

Battery

Bulb

Panasonic Panasonic

FILE

Tube of glue

Round patch

SUN SIGNALING MIRROR

Pin hole

Guide

FLOOR DEFLATING PLUG

Long patch

Line

POLYTHENE STORAGE BAGS

PRESSURE RELIEF VALVE BUNG

FIRST AID PACK

Line

Sinker

Blunt-tipped scissors

Hook

Emery paper

FISHING KIT

SPONGE

Mooring and anchoring

In most harbors and ports, a ship can moor (tie up or "make fast") directly to a pier, wharf, or quay (pronounced "key"), using heavy hawsers and docking lines attached to bitts or bollards. Hawsers are tied to each other with knots called bends. In open water, however, ships that are not under way must drop an anchor, which attaches the ship securely to the seabed. The earliest anchors were simply heavy stones. Later, various anchor designs were developed for different uses. Most small vessels today use Danforth or plow anchors, which dig deeply into the sea bottom. A permanent mooring is an anchor set in the bottom to which a ship can tie up without using its own anchor. On old sailing ships, anchors were pulled up, or "weighed," by sailors pushing against bars that turned a capstan, which wound up the anchor cable. Now, most capstans are powered by electricity.

STONE ANCHOR (KILLICK)

Rope hole

TYPES OF ANCHOR

CLOSE-STOWING ANCHOR

CQR ANCHOR (PLOW ANCHOR)

BRITISH ADMIRALTY ANCHOR TYPE ACII

YACHTSMAN'S ANCHOR (KEDGE)

STOCKLESS ANCHOR

MUSHROOM ANCHOR (PERMANENT MOORING ANCHOR)

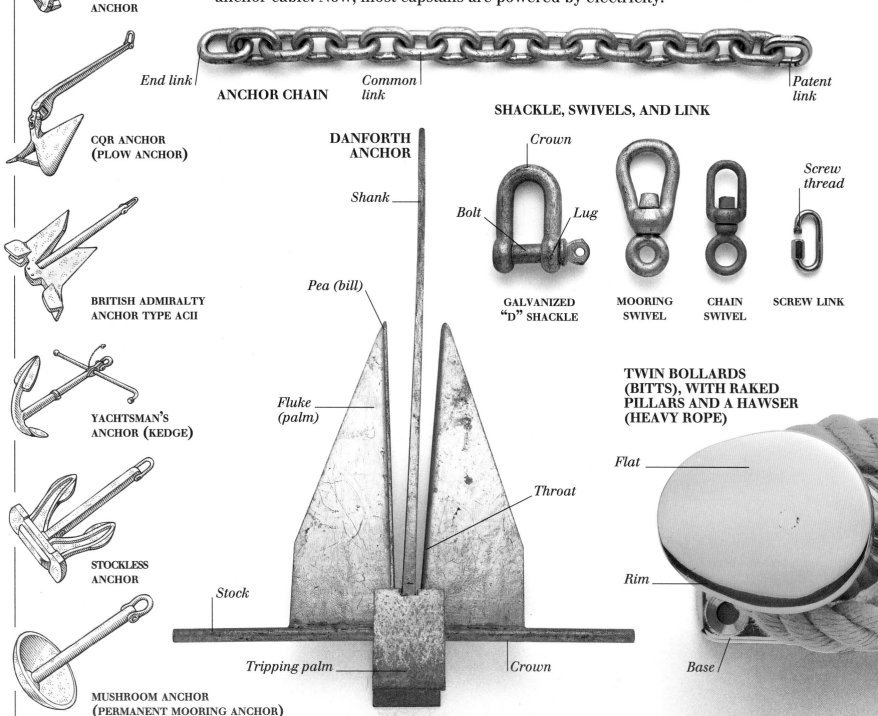

End link | *Common link* | *Patent link*

ANCHOR CHAIN

SHACKLE, SWIVELS, AND LINK

DANFORTH ANCHOR

Crown

Shank

Bolt *Lug*

Screw thread

Pea (bill)

GALVANIZED "D" SHACKLE | **MOORING SWIVEL** | **CHAIN SWIVEL** | **SCREW LINK**

Fluke (palm)

Throat

TWIN BOLLARDS (BITTS), WITH RAKED PILLARS AND A HAWSER (HEAVY ROPE)

Flat

Rim

Stock

Tripping palm *Crown*

Base

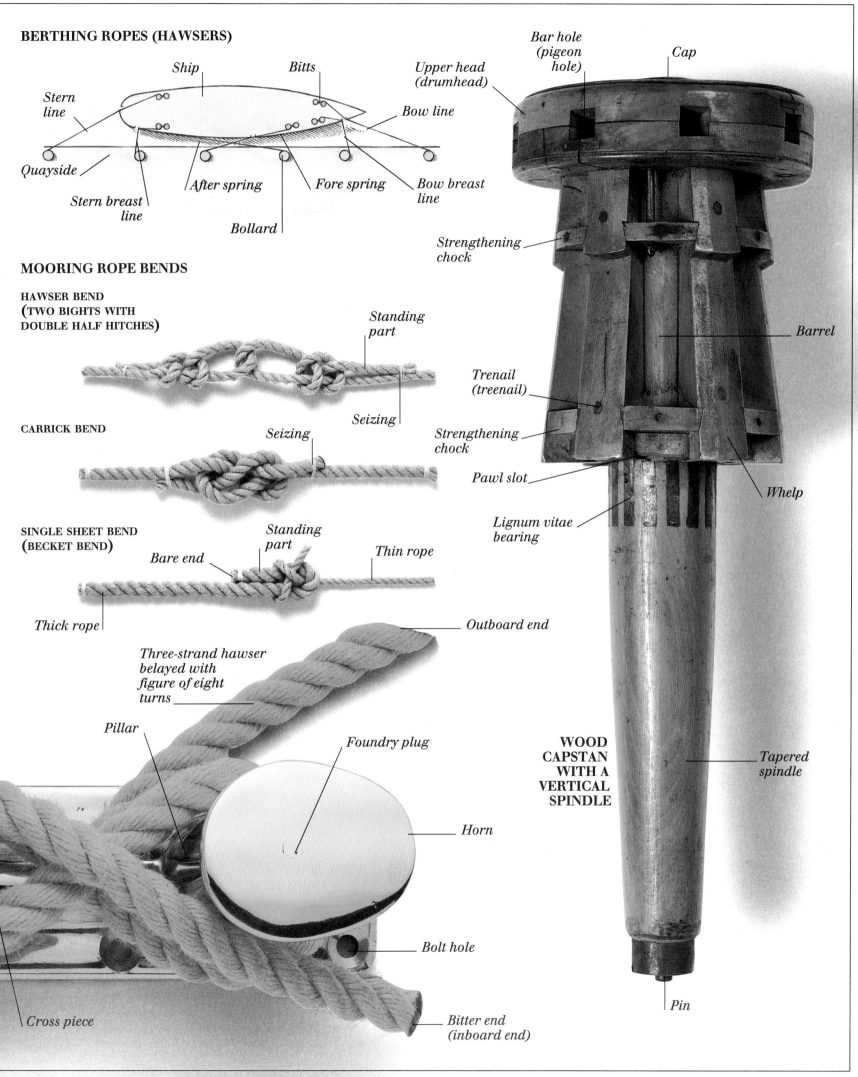

BERTHING ROPES (HAWSERS)

Stern line

Ship

Bitts

Upper head (drumhead)

Bar hole (pigeon hole)

Cap

Bow line

Quayside

Stern breast line

After spring

Fore spring

Bollard

Bow breast line

Strengthening chock

Barrel

MOORING ROPE BENDS

HAWSER BEND (TWO BIGHTS WITH DOUBLE HALF HITCHES)

Standing part

Seizing

CARRICK BEND

Seizing

SINGLE SHEET BEND (BECKET BEND)

Standing part

Bare end

Thin rope

Thick rope

Three-strand hawser belayed with figure of eight turns

Pillar

Outboard end

Foundry plug

Horn

Bolt hole

Cross piece

Bitter end (inboard end)

Trenail (treenail)

Strengthening chock

Pawl slot

Lignum vitae bearing

Whelp

WOOD CAPSTAN WITH A VERTICAL SPINDLE

Tapered spindle

Pin

Ropes and knots

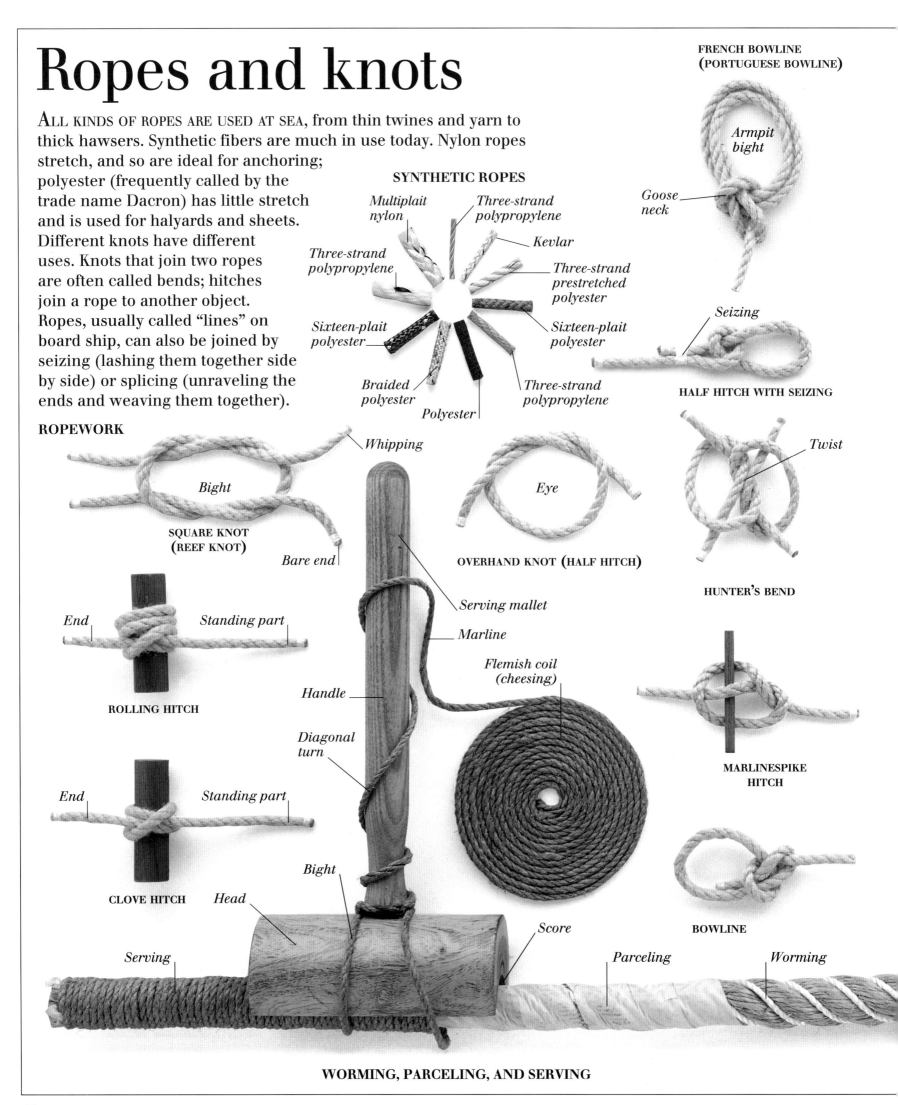

ALL KINDS OF ROPES ARE USED AT SEA, from thin twines and yarn to thick hawsers. Synthetic fibers are much in use today. Nylon ropes stretch, and so are ideal for anchoring; polyester (frequently called by the trade name Dacron) has little stretch and is used for halyards and sheets. Different knots have different uses. Knots that join two ropes are often called bends; hitches join a rope to another object. Ropes, usually called "lines" on board ship, can also be joined by seizing (lashing them together side by side) or splicing (unraveling the ends and weaving them together).

FRENCH BOWLINE (PORTUGUESE BOWLINE)

Armpit bight

Goose neck

Seizing

HALF HITCH WITH SEIZING

SYNTHETIC ROPES

Multiplait nylon

Three-strand polypropylene

Three-strand polypropylene

Kevlar

Three-strand prestretched polyester

Sixteen-plait polyester

Sixteen-plait polyester

Braided polyester

Three-strand polypropylene

Polyester

ROPEWORK

Whipping

Bight

SQUARE KNOT (REEF KNOT)

Bare end

Eye

OVERHAND KNOT (HALF HITCH)

Twist

HUNTER'S BEND

End

Standing part

ROLLING HITCH

Serving mallet

Marline

Flemish coil (cheesing)

MARLINESPIKE HITCH

Handle

End

Standing part

CLOVE HITCH

Head

Diagonal turn

Bight

Score

BOWLINE

Serving

Parceling

Worming

WORMING, PARCELING, AND SERVING

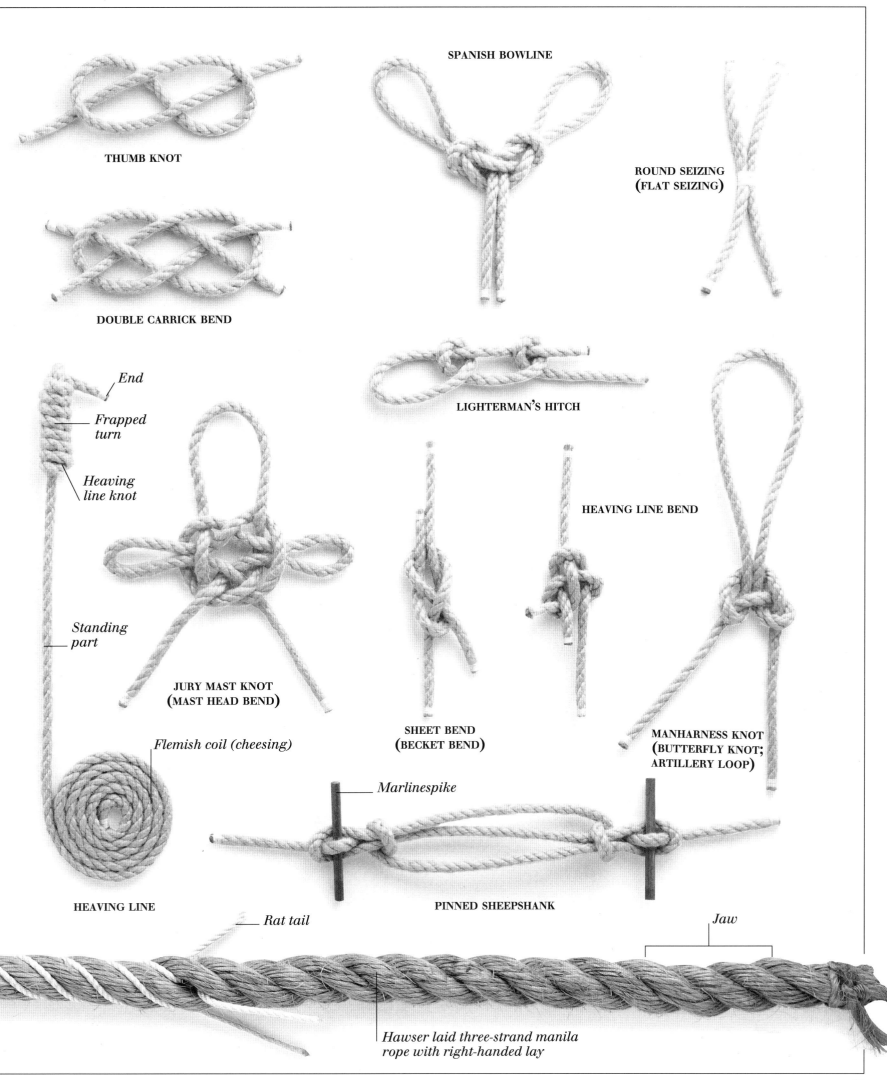

THUMB KNOT

SPANISH BOWLINE

ROUND SEIZING (FLAT SEIZING)

DOUBLE CARRICK BEND

End

Frapped turn

Heaving line knot

LIGHTERMAN'S HITCH

Standing part

HEAVING LINE BEND

JURY MAST KNOT (MAST HEAD BEND)

Flemish coil (cheesing)

SHEET BEND (BECKET BEND)

MANHARNESS KNOT (BUTTERFLY KNOT; ARTILLERY LOOP)

Marlinespike

HEAVING LINE

PINNED SHEEPSHANK

Jaw

Rat tail

Hawser laid three-strand manila rope with right-handed lay

49

Sailing clothing

THE PRINCIPAL FUNCTIONS OF SAILING CLOTHING are to maintain body temperature, be waterproof, and allow freedom of movement. The clothing shown is intended for long distance and foul-weather sailing. Water and wind both contribute to loss of body heat, and modern sailing clothing protects the body efficiently by allowing the formation of a layer of warm air around the body. The materials used must be lightweight and quick-drying. This jacket has numerous safety features, including life jacket, safety harness, whistle, and a pocket for emergency flares.

OLD-FASHIONED FOUL-WEATHER GEAR
Early life jackets were made of cork, or silky fibers known as kapok.

Cork life jacket

Kapok life jacket

Oilskin

Sou'wester

GLOVE

Water-resistant leather palm

Removable lining

Anti-seasickness wrist band

Adjustable storm cuff

High-intensity strobe light

OCEAN-SAILING TROUSERS

Suspenders

Webbing

Carabiner (double-action safety hook)

Life jacket pull tag

Chest-high handwarmer pocket

Nylon safety line

ACCESSORIES

Heavy-duty zipper

HAND WARMER

Metal casing

KNIFE AND SHEATH

Handle

SHACKLE PIN OPENER

Thigh pocket

Charcoal

Eye

Nylon reinforcement

Zinc cream

Applicator

SUN PROTECTION

Sheath

Blade

Marlinespike

DECK BOOT

DECK SHOES

Oiled leather upper

Watertight adjustable collar

Rot-proof synthetic thread

Nonslip sole

Adjustable ankle fastener

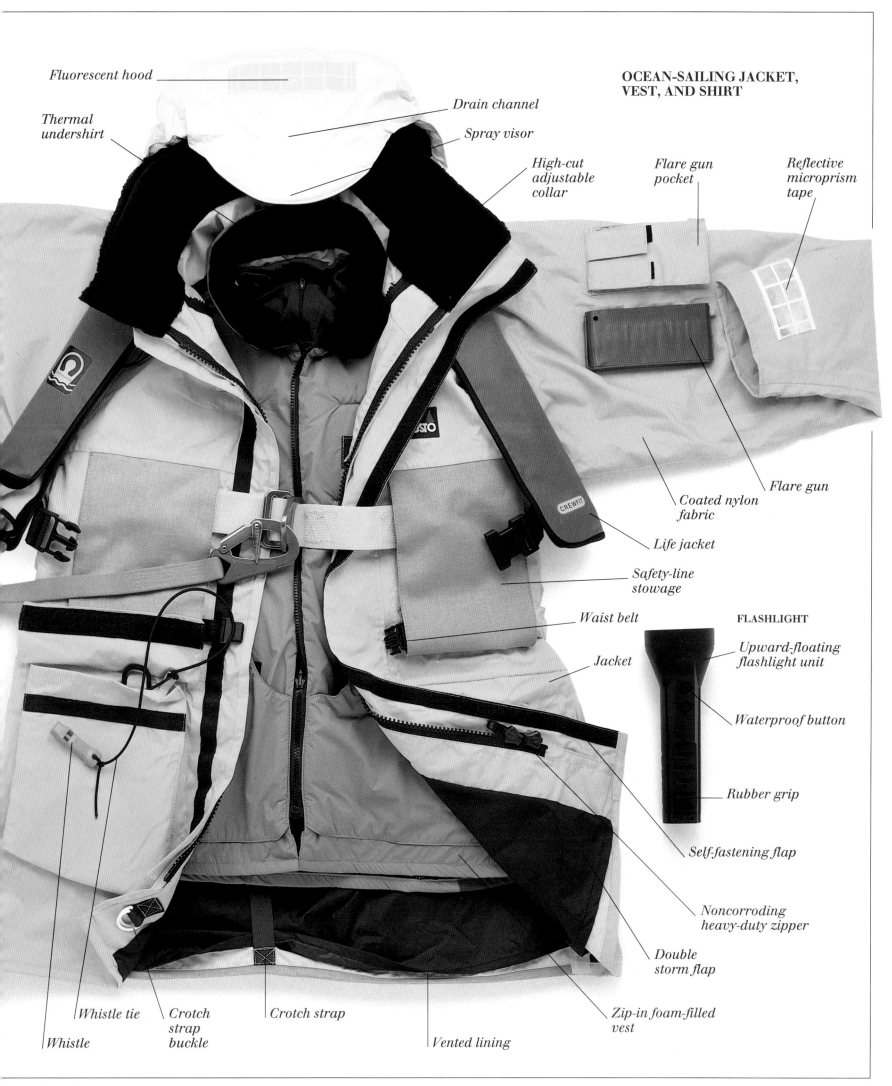

Fluorescent hood

Thermal
undershirt

Drain channel

Spray visor

OCEAN-SAILING JACKET,
VEST, AND SHIRT

High-cut
adjustable
collar

Flare gun
pocket

Reflective
microprism
tape

Flare gun

Coated nylon
fabric

Life jacket

Safety-line
stowage

Waist belt

FLASHLIGHT

Jacket

Upward-floating
flashlight unit

Waterproof button

Rubber grip

Self-fastening flap

Noncorroding
heavy-duty zipper

Double
storm flap

Zip-in foam-filled
vest

Whistle tie   Crotch
strap
buckle

Crotch strap

Vented lining

Whistle

51

The battleship

IN THE EARLY YEARS OF THE 20TH CENTURY, sea warfare—
attacking enemy vessels or defending a ship—was
revolutionized by the introduction of Dreadnought-type
battleships like the Brazilian vessel below. These new
ships combined the latest advances in steam
propulsion, gunnery, and armor plating. Their gun
turrets, protected by armor up to 12 in (30 cm) thick,
were designed to fire shells over great distances.
The ship shown here, the Minas Geraes, was 500 ft
(152 m) long. It was built at Elswick, England, and
launched in 1908. Its chief armament was of 12 in (30 cm)
guns (firing shells with a 12 in diameter). Other naval
weapons developed in the 20th century include the torpedo—
as portrayed on the upper cigarette card (right). This was
a self-propelled underwater missile, often steered by
gyro-control. Depth charges were designed in the
First World War for use against submerged U-boats.
They are canisters filled with explosives that are
detonated by depth-sensitive pistols. The lower
cigarette card shows depth charges being
fired by a "thrower", fired from a
torpedo tube, and rolled from the
stern. Ship's shields were fitted to
warships from the late 19th century
onwards. The shield shown
opposite depicts a traditional
ship's cannon.

Torpedo tube

Warhead

Sight

TORPEDOES

DEPTH
CHARGES

Side-thrown
canister

Stern-rolled
canister

Torpedo-fired
canister

Boat handling
derrick

BRAZILIAN BATTLESHIP

Rangefinder

Forward
funnel

Gunnery
spotting top

Light screen

Lifeboat

Purchase wire

Compass

Searchlight

Compass and rangefinder
platform

Searchlight
platform

Ship's wheel

Leading block

Tripod mast

Navigating bridge

Boat
winch

Conning tower

Captain's shelter/
chart house

Arms of
Brazil

Weather shutter
for gun

"F" turret

Jack staff

12 in (30 cm)
gun

Skylight

Stem
(false ram bow)

Porthole

Belt
armor

Forward
accommodation
ladder

Sighting
hood

"A" turret

Turret barbette

Open gun mounting

Steam launch

4.7 in (12 cm) gun

Guest boat boom

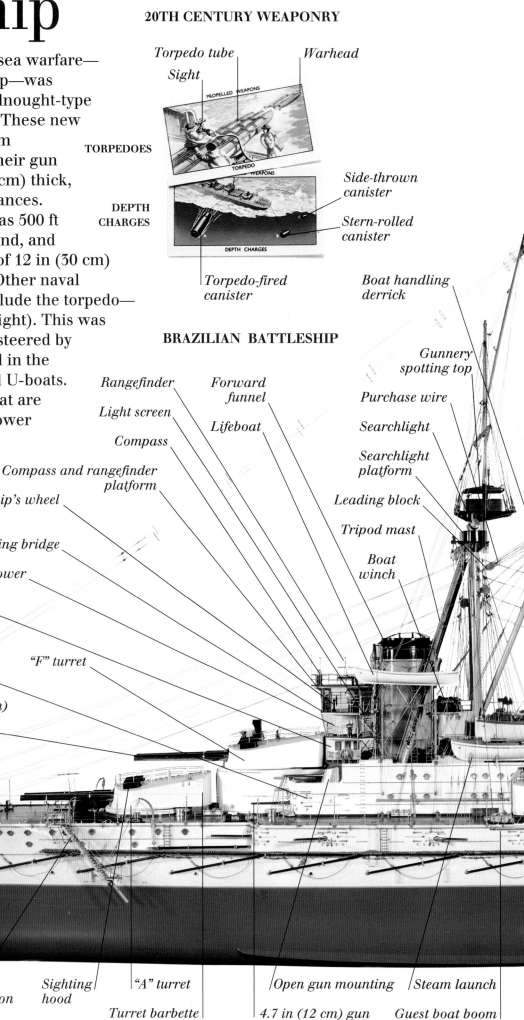

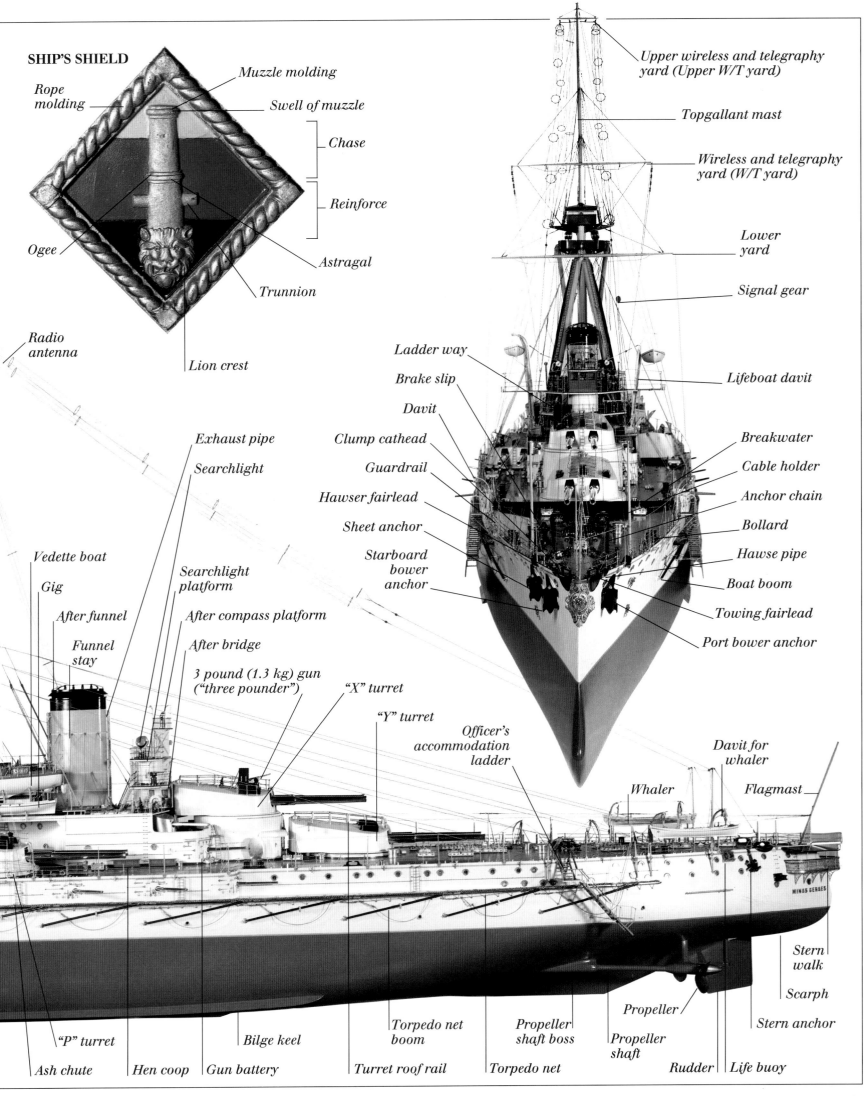

SHIP'S SHIELD

Rope molding

Muzzle molding

Swell of muzzle

Chase

Reinforce

Ogee

Astragal

Radio antenna

Trunnion

Lion crest

Upper wireless and telegraphy yard (Upper W/T yard)

Topgallant mast

Wireless and telegraphy yard (W/T yard)

Lower yard

Signal gear

Ladder way

Lifeboat davit

Brake slip

Davit

Clump cathead

Breakwater

Guardrail

Cable holder

Hawser fairlead

Anchor chain

Sheet anchor

Bollard

Starboard bower anchor

Hawse pipe

Boat boom

Towing fairlead

Port bower anchor

Exhaust pipe

Searchlight

Searchlight platform

After compass platform

After bridge

3 pound (1.3 kg) gun ("three pounder")

"X" turret

"Y" turret

Officer's accommodation ladder

Davit for whaler

Vedette boat

Gig

After funnel

Funnel stay

Whaler

Flagmast

"P" turret

Bilge keel

Torpedo net boom

Propeller shaft boss

Stern walk

Scarph

Propeller

Stern anchor

Ash chute

Hen coop

Gun battery

Turret roof rail

Torpedo net

Propeller shaft

Rudder

Life buoy

Fighting at sea

FROM THE MID-19TH CENTURY, ARMORED SHIPS provided a new challenge to enemy craft. In response, huge revolving gun turrets were developed. These could shoot in any direction, were loaded quickly from the breech, and fired exploding shells. Today's fighting ships, like the Royal Navy frigate opposite, also carry missile launchers and helicopters. Submarines operate underwater, have great speed, and some can fire missiles while submerged. A nuclear sub can operate for several years without refueling.

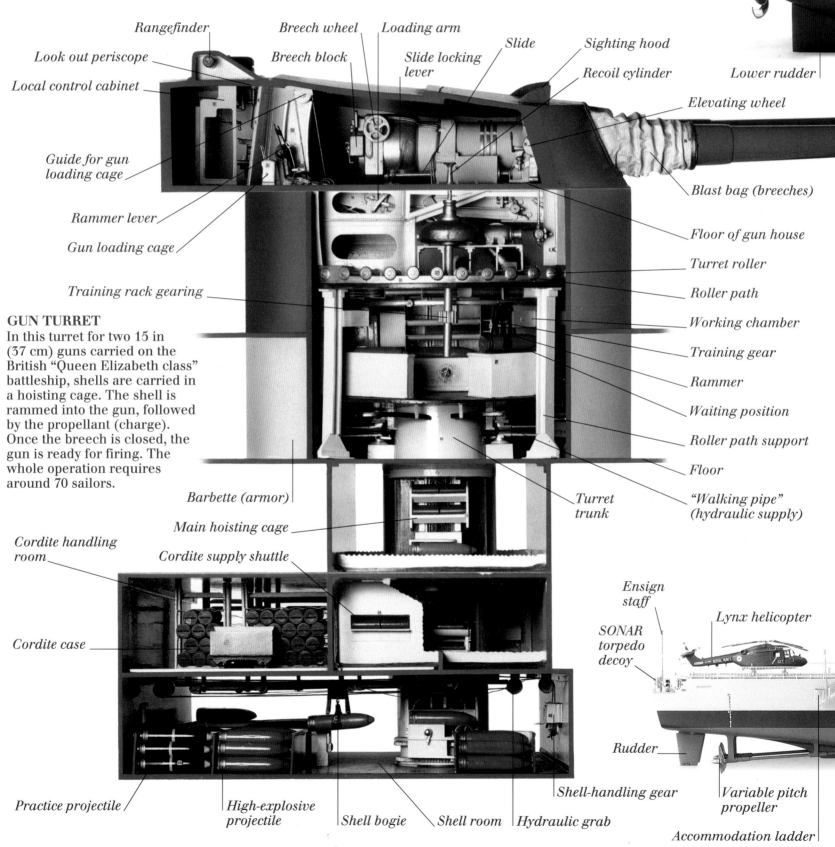

Stabilized fin

Aft hydroplane

Propeller

Lower rudder

Rangefinder

Breech wheel

Loading arm

Slide

Sighting hood

Look out periscope

Breech block

Slide locking lever

Recoil cylinder

Local control cabinet

Elevating wheel

Guide for gun loading cage

Blast bag (breeches)

Rammer lever

Floor of gun house

Gun loading cage

Turret roller

Training rack gearing

Roller path

GUN TURRET
In this turret for two 15 in (37 cm) guns carried on the British "Queen Elizabeth class" battleship, shells are carried in a hoisting cage. The shell is rammed into the gun, followed by the propellant (charge). Once the breech is closed, the gun is ready for firing. The whole operation requires around 70 sailors.

Working chamber

Training gear

Rammer

Waiting position

Roller path support

Floor

Barbette (armor)

Turret trunk

"Walking pipe" (hydraulic supply)

Main hoisting cage

Cordite handling room

Ensign staff

Cordite supply shuttle

Lynx helicopter

SONAR torpedo decoy

Cordite case

Rudder

Practice projectile

High-explosive projectile

Shell bogie

Shell room

Hydraulic grab

Shell-handling gear

Variable pitch propeller

Accommodation ladder

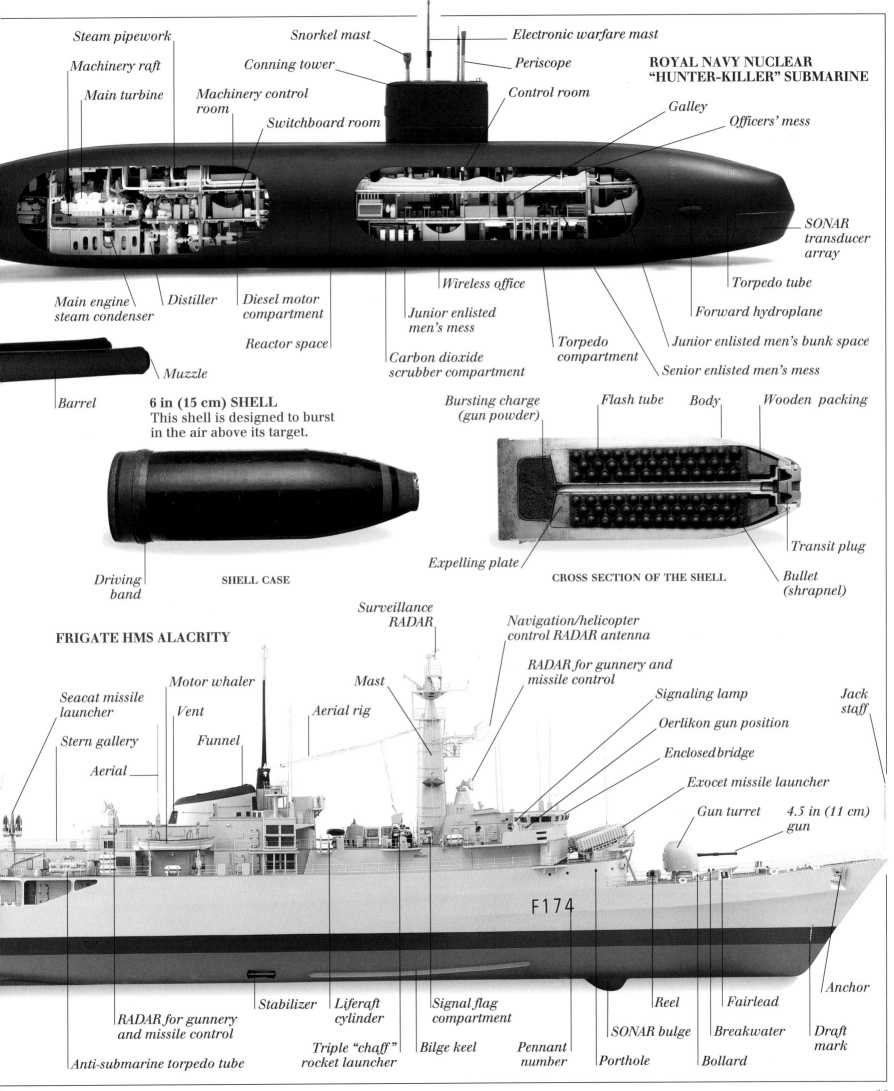

Steam pipework

Machinery raft

Main turbine

Machinery control room

Switchboard room

Snorkel mast

Conning tower

Periscope

Electronic warfare mast

Control room

ROYAL NAVY NUCLEAR "HUNTER-KILLER" SUBMARINE

Galley

Officers' mess

SONAR transducer array

Main engine steam condenser

Distiller

Muzzle

Barrel

Diesel motor compartment

Reactor space

Wireless office

Junior enlisted men's mess

Carbon dioxide scrubber compartment

Torpedo compartment

Torpedo tube

Forward hydroplane

Junior enlisted men's bunk space

Senior enlisted men's mess

6 in (15 cm) SHELL
This shell is designed to burst in the air above its target.

Bursting charge (gun powder)

Flash tube

Body

Wooden packing

Driving band

SHELL CASE

Expelling plate

CROSS SECTION OF THE SHELL

Transit plug

Bullet (shrapnel)

FRIGATE HMS ALACRITY

Surveillance RADAR

Navigation/helicopter control RADAR antenna

Motor whaler

Mast

RADAR for gunnery and missile control

Signaling lamp

Jack staff

Seacat missile launcher

Vent

Aerial rig

Oerlikon gun position

Stern gallery

Funnel

Enclosed bridge

Aerial

Exocet missile launcher

Gun turret

4.5 in (11 cm) gun

F174

RADAR for gunnery and missile control

Stabilizer

Liferaft cylinder

Signal flag compartment

Reel

Fairlead

Anchor

Anti-submarine torpedo tube

Triple "chaff" rocket launcher

Bilge keel

Pennant number

SONAR bulge

Breakwater

Draft mark

Porthole

Bollard

Fishing boats

From its origins thousands of years ago, when nets were dragged by hand through the water or hooks were hung from lines, fishing has developed into a great industry. By the late 19th century, fishing boats like the steam trawler shown here were ruthlessly efficient. Fleets of trawlers often served one factory ship which took the catch on board. Various types of net are used, including fixed traps, curtain-like drift nets, and funnel-shaped trawl nets. Nets can be laid at great speed with a netting needle. The catch is often gathered in baskets. Floats are arranged along the upper edge of a net to keep it buoyant. Modern technology makes tracing shoals of fish very easy. SONAR (SOund Navigation And Ranging) fish finders, for example, can even show the whereabouts of individual fish at the push of a button.

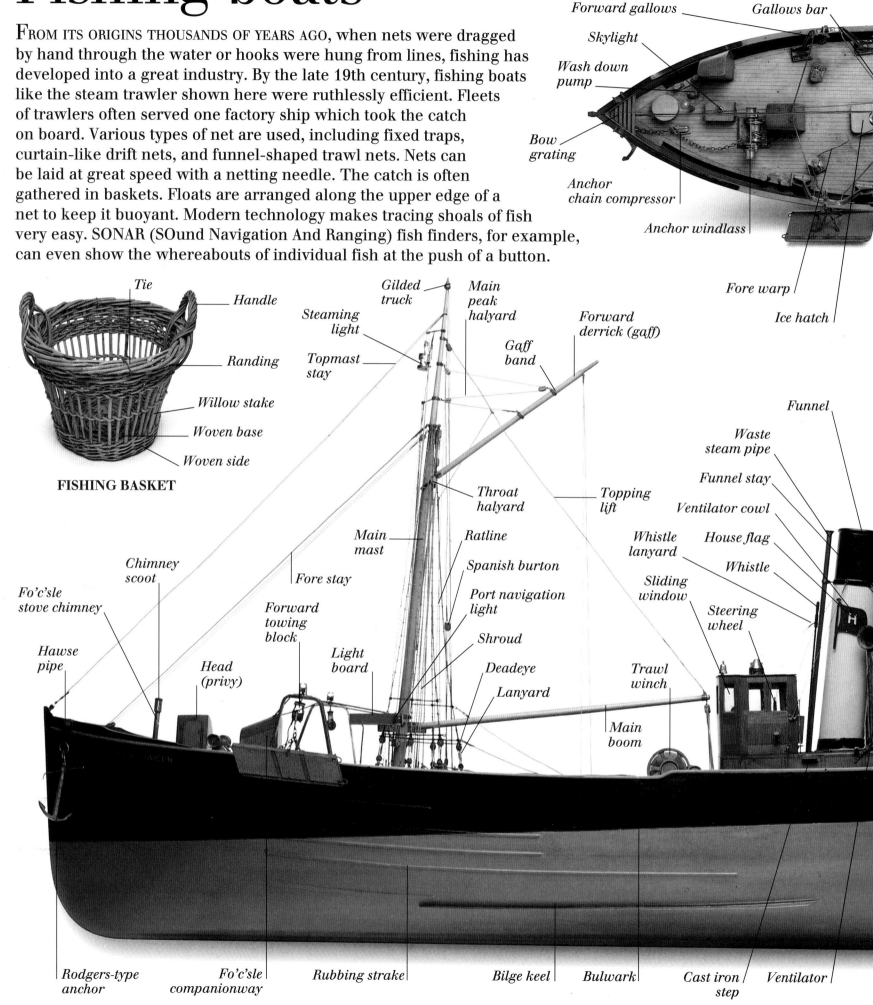

STEAM TRAWLER (DECK VIEW)

Forward gallows

Gallows bar

Skylight

Wash down pump

Bow grating

Anchor chain compressor

Anchor windlass

Fore warp

Ice hatch

Tie

Handle

Randing

Willow stake

Woven base

Woven side

FISHING BASKET

Gilded truck

Steaming light

Topmast stay

Main peak halyard

Forward derrick (gaff)

Gaff band

Throat halyard

Topping lift

Funnel

Waste steam pipe

Funnel stay

Ventilator cowl

House flag

Whistle

Whistle lanyard

Sliding window

Steering wheel

Main mast

Ratline

Spanish burton

Port navigation light

Shroud

Deadeye

Lanyard

Trawl winch

Main boom

Chimney scoot

Fo'c'sle stove chimney

Fore stay

Forward towing block

Light board

Hawse pipe

Head (privy)

Rodgers-type anchor

Fo'c'sle companionway

Rubbing strake

Bilge keel

Bulwark

Cast iron step

Ventilator

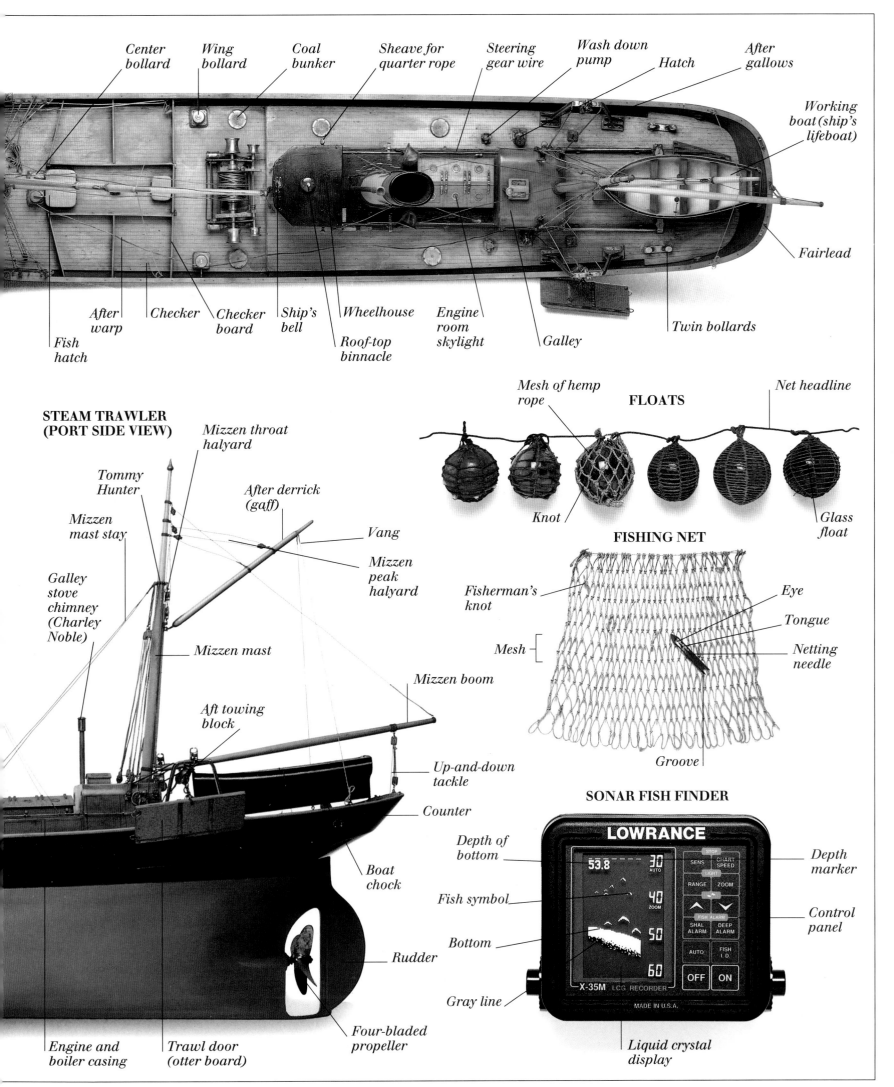

Center bollard

Wing bollard

Coal bunker

Sheave for quarter rope

Steering gear wire

Wash down pump

Hatch

After gallows

Working boat (ship's lifeboat)

Fairlead

After warp

Checker

Checker board

Ship's bell

Wheelhouse

Roof-top binnacle

Engine room skylight

Galley

Twin bollards

Fish hatch

STEAM TRAWLER (PORT SIDE VIEW)

Mizzen throat halyard

Tommy Hunter

After derrick (gaff)

Vang

Mizzen mast stay

Mizzen peak halyard

Galley stove chimney (Charley Noble)

Mizzen mast

Aft towing block

Mizzen boom

Up-and-down tackle

Counter

Boat chock

Engine and boiler casing

Trawl door (otter board)

Rudder

Four-bladed propeller

Mesh of hemp rope

FLOATS

Net headline

Knot

Glass float

FISHING NET

Fisherman's knot

Eye

Tongue

Mesh

Netting needle

Groove

SONAR FISH FINDER

Depth of bottom

Depth marker

Fish symbol

Control panel

Bottom

Gray line

Liquid crystal display

LOWRANCE

53.8

X-35M LCG RECORDER

MADE IN U.S.A.

Under the sea

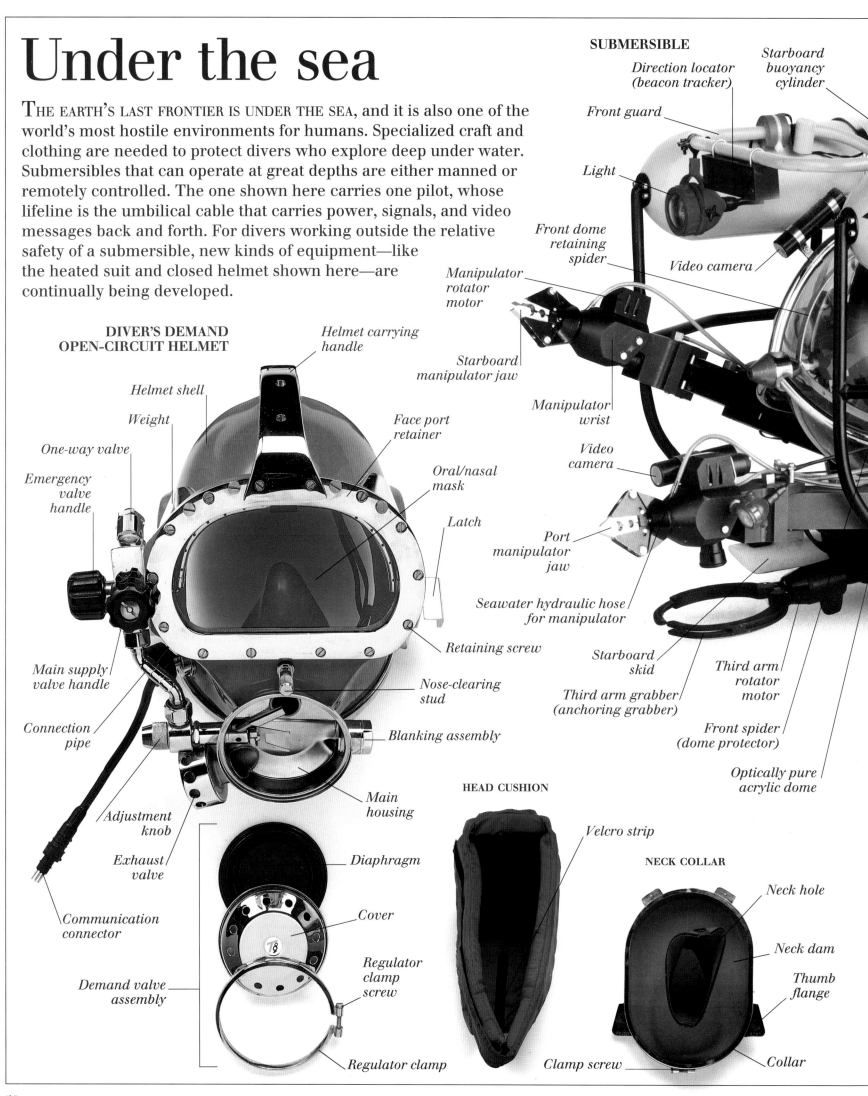

THE EARTH'S LAST FRONTIER IS UNDER THE SEA, and it is also one of the world's most hostile environments for humans. Specialized craft and clothing are needed to protect divers who explore deep under water. Submersibles that can operate at great depths are either manned or remotely controlled. The one shown here carries one pilot, whose lifeline is the umbilical cable that carries power, signals, and video messages back and forth. For divers working outside the relative safety of a submersible, new kinds of equipment—like the heated suit and closed helmet shown here—are continually being developed.

SUBMERSIBLE

Direction locator (beacon tracker)

Starboard buoyancy cylinder

Front guard

Light

Front dome retaining spider

Video camera

Manipulator rotator motor

Starboard manipulator jaw

Manipulator wrist

Video camera

Port manipulator jaw

Seawater hydraulic hose for manipulator

Starboard skid

Third arm grabber (anchoring grabber)

Third arm rotator motor

Front spider (dome protector)

Optically pure acrylic dome

DIVER'S DEMAND OPEN-CIRCUIT HELMET

Helmet carrying handle

Helmet shell

Weight

One-way valve

Emergency valve handle

Face port retainer

Oral/nasal mask

Latch

Main supply valve handle

Connection pipe

Retaining screw

Nose-clearing stud

Blanking assembly

Main housing

Adjustment knob

Exhaust valve

Diaphragm

Cover

Regulator clamp screw

Communication connector

Demand valve assembly

Regulator clamp

HEAD CUSHION

Velcro strip

NECK COLLAR

Neck hole

Neck dam

Thumb flange

Clamp screw

Collar

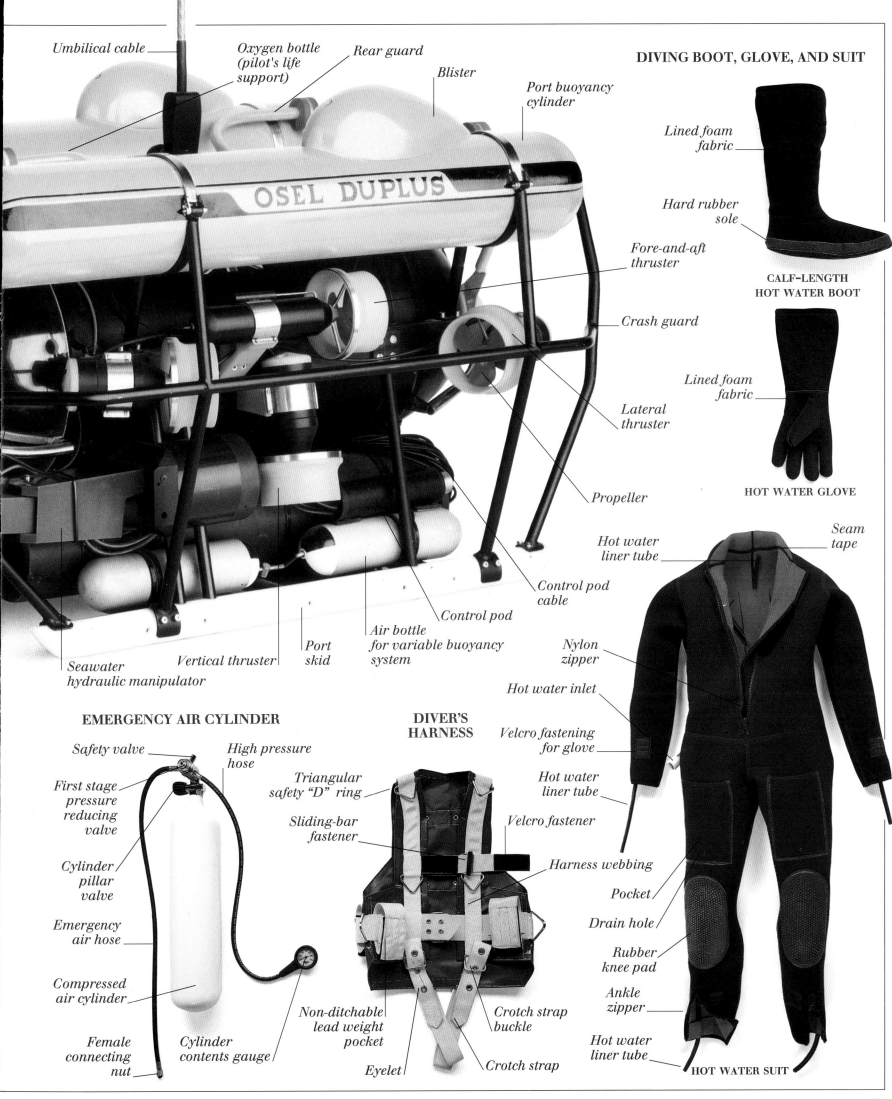

Umbilical cable

Oxygen bottle (pilot's life support)

Rear guard

Blister

Port buoyancy cylinder

OSEL DUPLUS

Fore-and-aft thruster

Crash guard

Lateral thruster

Propeller

Control pod cable

Control pod

Air bottle for variable buoyancy system

Seawater hydraulic manipulator

Vertical thruster

Port skid

DIVING BOOT, GLOVE, AND SUIT

Lined foam fabric

Hard rubber sole

CALF-LENGTH HOT WATER BOOT

Lined foam fabric

HOT WATER GLOVE

Seam tape

Hot water liner tube

Nylon zipper

Hot water inlet

Velcro fastening for glove

Hot water liner tube

Velcro fastener

Harness webbing

Pocket

Drain hole

Rubber knee pad

Ankle zipper

Hot water liner tube

HOT WATER SUIT

EMERGENCY AIR CYLINDER

Safety valve

High pressure hose

First stage pressure reducing valve

Cylinder pillar valve

Emergency air hose

Compressed air cylinder

Female connecting nut

Cylinder contents gauge

DIVER'S HARNESS

Triangular safety "D" ring

Sliding-bar fastener

Non-ditchable lead weight pocket

Eyelet

Crotch strap buckle

Crotch strap

59

Index

Acknowledgments

Dorling Kindersley would like to thank:
Geoff Hales and Harvey B. Loomis for advice;
David Spence, Gillian Hutchinson, David
Topliss, Simon Stephens, Robert Baldwin,
Jonathan Betts, all of the National Maritime
Museum, London; Ian Friel; Simon Turnage of
Captain O.M. Watts of London Ltd., for sailing
equipment; Davey and Company Ltd., Great
Dunmow, for marine equipment; Avon
Inflatables Ltd., Llanelli; Musto Ltd., Benfleet,
for sailing clothing; Peter Martin of Spencer
Rigging Ltd., Southampton; Peter Rowson of
Ratseys Sailmakers, Southampton; Swiftech
Ltd., Wallingford; Colin Scattergood of the
Barrow Boat Company Ltd., Colchester; Tim
Spalton of Glyn Locke (Racing Shells) Ltd.,
Chalgrove; Professor J.S. Morrison of the
Trireme Trust, Cambridge; The Cutty Sark
Maritime Trust; Adrian Daniels of Kelvin
Hughes Marine Instruments, London; Arthur
Credland of Hull City Council Museums and Art
Galleries; The Hull Maritime Society; Gerald
Clark for knots; Peter Fitzgerald of the Science

Museum, London; Alec Michael of HMB
Subwork Ltd., Great Yarmouth, and Ray Ward
of the OSEL Group, Great Yarmouth, for access
to submersible; Richard Bird of UWI,
Weybridge, for diving equipment; Walker
Marine Instruments, Birmingham; The
International Sailing Craft Association; The
Exeter Maritime Museum; Jane Wilson of the
Trinity Lighthouse Company, London; The
Imperial War Museum Collections; Daniel
Bombigher; Thorn Security Ltd.; Michael Bach

Additional design assistance:
Nick Jackson, Johnny Pau

Additional editorial assistance:
Susan Bosanko, Deirdre Clark, Paul Docherty,
David Harding, Edwina Johnson, Gail Lawther,
Louise Tucker

Illustrators:
Roy Flooks, Linden Artists, John Woodcock

Model makers:
Richard Kemp, Kelvin Thatcher, Paul
Wilkinson

Picture credits:
b=bottom, t=top, l=left, r=right
British Museum page 8bl; Michael Holford 10tr;
National Maritime Museum 13br, 20-21b

The nautical chart on page 39 is Crown
Copyright reproduced from Admiralty Charts/
Publications with the permission of the
controller of Her Majesty's Stationery Office.

Picture research:
Clive Webster